Practice Exams with Visual Guides and "Try It!" Exercises

for

Coon's

Psychology: A Journey

Second Edition

Practice Exams by
Britton Mace
Southern Utah University

Visual Guides by
Art VanDeventer
Thomas Nelson Community College

THOMSON
WADSWORTH

Australia • Canada • Mexico • Singapore • Spain • United Kingdom • United States

Printed in the United States of America
1 2 3 4 5 6 7   07 06 05 04

Printer: Malloy Incorporated

0-534-63268-8

For more information about our products, contact us at:
Thomson Learning Academic Resource Center
1-800-423-0563

For permission to use material from this text or product, submit a request online at
http://www.thomsonrights.com
Any additional questions about permissions can be submitted at
thomsonrights@thomson.com

Thomson Wadsworth
10 Davis Drive
Belmont, CA 94002-3098
USA

Asia
Thomson Learning
5 Shenton Way #01-01
UIC Building
Singapore 068808

Australia/New Zealand
Thomson Learning
102 Dodds Street
Southbank, Victoria 3006
Australia

Canada
Nelson
1120 Birchmount Road
Toronto, Ontario M1K 5G4
Canada

Europe/Middle East/South Africa
Thomson Learning
High Holborn House
50/51 Bedford Row
London WC1R 4LR
United Kingdom

Latin America
Thomson Learning
Seneca, 53
Colonia Polanco
11560 Mexico D.F.
Mexico

Spain/Portugal
Paraninfo
Calle/Magallanes, 25
28015 Madrid, Spain

Table of Contents

About the Visual Guides

Research has shown that presenting information in a visual format improves retention of material for some learners. The visual guides began several years ago with an individual instructor's attempt to give students a study tool in an alternative format that allowed them to review information as they prepared for examinations. Many of you will find the visual guides extremely helpful from the very beginning of your course. Others of you will discover their value as you proceed with your studies.

How do you make use of these visual guides? These visual guides can be an integral part of your preparation to study, the reading and studying of the material, and the preparation for testing.

SURVEY: Begin your preparations by surveying the visual guides. A preview like this gives you an overview of what material will be covered and highlights some key concepts you will wish to give special attention. Then survey the chapter to get an even more detailed idea of what the chapter contains. Seeing how each topic in the text leads to another topic helps your understanding of the chapter progression. Now, read the chapter in detail.

RELATE: The visual presentation demonstrates how one key topic relates to another. You may be surprised to see how many concepts are inter-connected, and the visual guides provide an overview of these connections. Your long-term retention of the material can be improved by having an understanding of how the material you are studying relates to other material. The material is generally laid out in a top-down, left-to-right format. However, as you will see, the fact that most concepts are interrelated makes the exact layout of no great consequence.

REVIEW: After you have read the chapter and want to test your mastery of the material, use the visual guides for review. At each point along the material, ask yourself:
- How much you now know about each topic that you find discussed there?
- What information do you now know that was not included in the visual guide?
- What items would you have added if you had been the visual guide creator?
- What questions is your instructor likely to ask about the topics that have been presented?

Some students may find it helpful to make detailed notes directly on the visual guides as they progress through the chapters.

Art VanDeventer

About the Authors

Art VanDeventer is currently the Head of the Psychology Department at Thomas Nelson Community College in Hampton, Virginia. During active military service he attained a Master of Arts in counseling psychology from Chapman University. He has served internships in both public and private psychiatric hospital settings. He has worked in in-patient adolescent psychiatric settings and as a university administrator. Since 1988 he worked as an adjunct faculty member teaching psychology until taking a full-time position on faculty at Thomas Nelson in 1999. The visual guides in this booklet are an outgrowth of the cognitive maps that he created as study guides to assist his students in mastering the material in introductory psychology classes.

Britton L. Mace is an Associate Professor of Psychology at Southern Utah University. Britt teaches classes in general, environmental, social, and cognitive psychology. His research interests include the psychological consequences of noise exposure, the human-environment relationship, environmental education, and the valuation of public goods. Britt resides near Zion National Park and enjoys exploring the beautiful canyons with his wife and two sons.

Chapter 1 – Introduction to Psychology and Research Methods

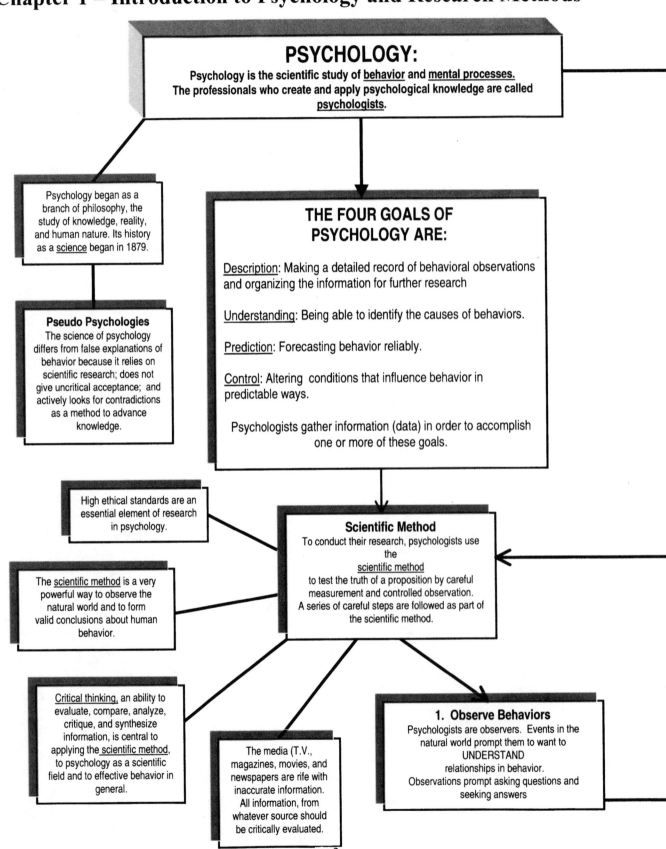

PSYCHOLOGY:
Psychology is the scientific study of <u>behavior</u> and <u>mental processes.</u>
The professionals who create and apply psychological knowledge are called
<u>psychologists</u>.

Psychology began as a branch of philosophy, the study of knowledge, reality, and human nature. Its history as a <u>science</u> began in 1879.

Pseudo Psychologies
The science of psychology differs from false explanations of behavior because it relies on scientific research; does not give uncritical acceptance; and actively looks for contradictions as a method to advance knowledge.

THE FOUR GOALS OF PSYCHOLOGY ARE:

<u>Description</u>: Making a detailed record of behavioral observations and organizing the information for further research

<u>Understanding</u>: Being able to identify the causes of behaviors.

<u>Prediction</u>: Forecasting behavior reliably.

<u>Control</u>: Altering conditions that influence behavior in predictable ways.

Psychologists gather information (data) in order to accomplish one or more of these goals.

High ethical standards are an essential element of research in psychology.

The <u>scientific method</u> is a very powerful way to observe the natural world and to form valid conclusions about human behavior.

Scientific Method
To conduct their research, psychologists use the
<u>scientific method</u>
to test the truth of a proposition by careful measurement and controlled observation.
A series of careful steps are followed as part of the scientific method.

<u>Critical thinking</u>, an ability to evaluate, compare, analyze, critique, and synthesize information, is central to applying the <u>scientific method</u>, to psychology as a scientific field and to effective behavior in general.

The media (T.V., magazines, movies, and newspapers are rife with inaccurate information. All information, from whatever source should be critically evaluated.

1. Observe Behaviors
Psychologists are observers. Events in the natural world prompt them to want to
UNDERSTAND
relationships in behavior.
Observations prompt asking questions and seeking answers

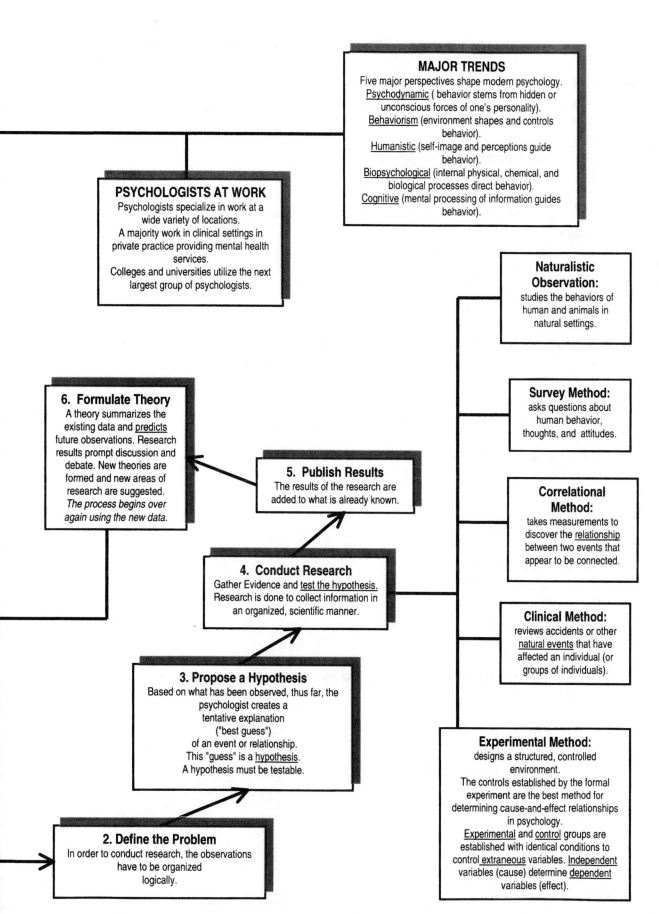

MAJOR TRENDS

Five major perspectives shape modern psychology.
Psychodynamic (behavior stems from hidden or unconscious forces of one's personality).
Behaviorism (environment shapes and controls behavior).
Humanistic (self-image and perceptions guide behavior).
Biopsychological (internal physical, chemical, and biological processes direct behavior).
Cognitive (mental processing of information guides behavior).

PSYCHOLOGISTS AT WORK

Psychologists specialize in work at a wide variety of locations.
A majority work in clinical settings in private practice providing mental health services.
Colleges and universities utilize the next largest group of psychologists.

Naturalistic Observation:
studies the behaviors of human and animals in natural settings.

Survey Method:
asks questions about human behavior, thoughts, and attitudes.

Correlational Method:
takes measurements to discover the relationship between two events that appear to be connected.

Clinical Method:
reviews accidents or other natural events that have affected an individual (or groups of individuals).

Experimental Method:
designs a structured, controlled environment.
The controls established by the formal experiment are the best method for determining cause-and-effect relationships in psychology.
Experimental and control groups are established with identical conditions to control extraneous variables. Independent variables (cause) determine dependent variables (effect).

6. Formulate Theory
A theory summarizes the existing data and predicts future observations. Research results prompt discussion and debate. New theories are formed and new areas of research are suggested.
The process begins over again using the new data.

5. Publish Results
The results of the research are added to what is already known.

4. Conduct Research
Gather Evidence and test the hypothesis.
Research is done to collect information in an organized, scientific manner.

3. Propose a Hypothesis
Based on what has been observed, thus far, the psychologist creates a tentative explanation ("best guess") of an event or relationship.
This "guess" is a hypothesis.
A hypothesis must be testable.

2. Define the Problem
In order to conduct research, the observations have to be organized logically.

Chapter 1:
Introduction to Psychology and Research Methods

Practice Exam

1. Psychology is defined as the scientific study of _____ .
   a. human behavior
   b. the mind
   c. behavior and mental processes
   d. mental processes

2. A psychologist whose interests lie in reasoning, problem solving, and memory is probably a
   a. developmental psychologist.
   b. learning psychologist.
   c. social psychologist.
   d. cognitive psychologist.

3. Introspection turned out to be a poor way to answer many questions because
   a. Wundt would not allow others to use it without permission.
   b. structuralists frequently disagreed.
   c. functionalists frequently disagreed.
   d. it only examined perception.

4. Behaviorism is the study of
   a. covert behavior.
   b. consciousness.
   c. overt, observable behavior.
   d. introspection.

5. Humanism stresses
   a. unconscious forces.
   b. free will.
   c. environmental control.
   d. determinism.

6. Who among the following would be most likely to have special training in the theories and therapy of Freud?
   a. psychiatrist
   b. psychologist
   c. psychoanalyst
   d. clinical psychologist

7. Behaviorism helped make psychology a
   a. fad.
   b. science.
   c. specialty.
   d. hoax.

8. Which of the following is stressed in the professional code of ethics?
   a. personal morality
   b. high levels of competition
   c. respect for people's right to privacy
   d. research protocols with humans only

9. A researcher looking for a way to improve children's math learning would most likely engage in what kind of research?
   a. basic
   b. applied
   c. pure
   d. group dynamics

10. Which of the following can legally prescribe drugs?
    a. psychiatrist
    b. clinical psychologist
    c. counseling psychologist
    d. psychiatric social workers

11. People who believe that a new diet is safe and effective because a doctor wrote the book are forgetting which of the following principles?
    a. Few "truths" transcend the need for testing.
    b. Evidence varies in quality.
    c. Authority does not automatically make an idea true.
    d. Critical thinking requires an open mind.

12. Which of the following terms refers to the tentative explanation of a relationship (event)?
    a. hypothesis
    b. operational definition
    c. theory
    d. observation

13. Which of the following is an advantage of the correlational method?
    a. high degree of control
    b. allows prediction
    c. not susceptible to coincidence
    d. confirms cause-and-effect

14. Dr. Bensko is investigating the effects of violent cartoon programs on children's aggressive play behavior. She has one group of 4-year-olds watch a 30-minute tape of a children's cartoon containing violence and another group of children the same age watch a non-violent cartoon for the same length of time. Then she has trained observers watch the children at play and obtain aggression scores for each child. In this example, the dependent variable is
   a.   the aggression scores.
   b.   the violent tape.
   c.   the non-violent tape.
   d.   the 4-year-olds.

15. Compared with other methods, an advantage of naturalistic observation is that
   a.   causes of behavior can be identified.
   b.   behavior has not been tampered with by outside sources.
   c.   the extent of the correlation between events can be carefully estimated.
   d.   hypotheses derived from theories can be appropriately tested.

16. A field experiment
   a.   takes place in a field.
   b.   is done in a real-world setting.
   c.   often produces artificial behavior.
   d.   is more tightly controlled than an experiment in the laboratory.

17. Joe takes an herbal supplement for pain in his knees. A few days after starting the supplement, his pain seems to decrease, and he tells people that this supplement is wonderful at controlling knee pain. What else could explain Joe's diminished pain?
   a.   the placebo effect
   b.   the replication effect
   c.   the experimenter effect
   d.   the observer effect

18. If neither the subjects nor the experimenter know which subjects get the true independent variable and which get the placebo, the study is called a _____ experiment.
   a.   single-blind
   b.   double-blind
   c.   field
   d.   dual

19. Dr. White wants to find out how middle class America feels about taxes. She goes to Neiman-Marcus and surveys the customers there. What has she done wrong?
   a.   She is questioning the government.
   b.   She needed to have written questions.
   c.   She failed to get a representative sample.
   d.   She fell victim to the placebo effect.

20.   Which of the following is one of the three major ethical issues to which researchers must be sensitive?
    a.   deception
    b.   financial burden
    c.   inconsequential harm
    d.   invasion of personal beliefs

Try It!

The purpose of this exercise is to help you learn what psychology is about and to impress on you that what psychologists are doing is often different from the popular notions held by persons who are not familiar with what psychologists study. You probably had some of the same misconceptions before beginning this course. Begin by reading Chapter 1 of the text. Look for the definition of psychology given on page 1 and write it down so that you can complete this assignment. Then follow directions, record responses, and discuss what you find.

1. Ask five people what they think psychology is. Ask each to give a brief statement about what it is or what psychologists study. Select a variety of people. They should be persons of different ages, sexes, and educational levels.

2. Record pertinent data about each subject (sex, approximate age, educational level) and the verbatim response to your question. Do not add to the response or try to clarify it.

3. After you have collected all your responses, do an analysis, comparing what you were told by the respondents with the definition in the text. The questions on page 9 should help you in your analysis.

What is Psychology? Data Sheet:

Name _____

Subject #1   Sex_____   Age (approx.)_____   Education_____

Subject #2   Sex_____   Age (approx.)_____   Education_____

Subject #3   Sex_____   Age (approx.)_____   Education_____

Subject #4   Sex_____   Age (approx.)_____   Education_____

Subject #5   Sex_____   Age (approx.)_____   Education_____

What is Psychology? Analysis of Responses:

A. The definition of psychology given in your text is:

B. What are some of the common elements in the statements made by your subjects?

C. How do the popular notions about psychology given by your subjects differ from the definition given in the text?

D. What are some of the major misconceptions that your subjects had about psychology?

Try It!

Consider the following questions related to the scientific method and experimental design. In answering these, consider what you have learned about surveys and other non-experimental data collection tools. If you were a researcher interested in studying temperature and aggression, how would the following issues affect your investigations?

A. What are the advantages and disadvantages of Internet Surveys?

B. If you could only ask three questions in a psychological survey, what would they be?

C. What population would you be interested in studying?

D. How would you obtain a valid sample?

E. Is it likely that any of your questions would be affected by a bias?

Chapter 2 - The Brain, Biology and Behavior

BIOPSYCHOLOGY
Psychologists who study how processes in the body, brain, and nervous system relate to behavior are called biopsychologists.

ENDOCRINE SYSTEM
Endocrine glands utilize chemicals called hormones as the second largest communication system within the body. Behavior is greatly influenced by the ebb and flow of hormones in the bloodstream.

NERVES
Bundles of neuron fibers carrying messages throughout the body create nerves and nervous systems.

PERIPHERAL NERVOUS SYSTEM
The Peripheral Nervous System (PNS) consists of all parts of the nervous system outside the CNS.

CENTRAL NERVOUS SYSTEM
The brain and the spinal column form the Central Nervous System (CNS).
Seventy percent of the neurons in the CNS are found in the brain.

NEURONS
Ultimately all behavior can be traced to the activity of nerve cells. Nerve cells (neurons) send messages throughout the body by combining chemical, biological and electrical elements. The various parts of neurons have specific functions.

SOMATIC NERVOUS SYSTEM
Messages from the sense organs and skeletal muscles travel along the somatic nervous system to the CNS.

NEUROGENESIS
Recent research indicates the brain's circuitry is not static.
The brain grows new nerve cells and it can "rewire" itself in response to changing environmental conditions.

DENDRITES
Messages are received from direct stimulation or chemical transmission from other neurons.

HEMISPHERES & HANDEDNESS
Whether you are right-handed, left-handed, or ambidextrous is determined in the brain.
Ninety percent of people are right-handed.
Speech is a left-brain function. Ninety-four percent of humans use the left hemisphere for language.
Sixty-eight percent of left-handers produce language in the left hemisphere.

CELL BODY (SOMA)
The soma receives messages from other cells and sends messages of its own (nerve impulses).

AUTONOMIC NERVOUS SYSTEM
Messages to and from the internal organs and glands are carried along the autonomic nervous system (ANS). The sympathetic branch of the ANS arouses the body, while the parasympathetic branch calms the body.

AXON FIBERS
Messages are carried away from the soma along the axon fibers.

AXON TERMINALS
Branching fibers at the end of the axon store neurotransmitters for release.

NEUROTRANSMITTERS
Chemicals that are released by a neuron across the synaptic gap in order to alter activity of other neurons are neurotransmitters.
Some neurotransmitters cause excitation of the next neuron while others may inhibit the post-synaptic neuron.

RECORDINGS & IMAGES

Bioelectrical recordings and computer-generated images of brain activity
give additional insight into how the brain works.

OTHER TECHNIQUES

Ablation (surgical removal of portions of the brain),
Deep Lesioning (destroying brain tissue with an electrode), and
Electrical Stimulation of the brain provide added understanding of brain's function.

BRAIN MAPPING

In order to determine how the brain works, biopsychologists attempt to determine which areas of the brain are responsible for specific behaviors by mapping the brain.
Functions of the brain are mapped by activating or disabling specific areas of the brain and observing whether behaviors cease, continue, or change.

CASE STUDIES

Changes in personality, behavior or sensation of individuals who have suffered brain injury or disease frequently offer insight into brain function.

CEREBRUM

Two large hemispheres (the cerebrum) cover the upper part of the brain. The cerebral cortex (the outer layer of the cerebrum) is responsible for most higher mental functions such as sensation (sight, hearing, touch, and movement).

THE BRAIN

The largest center of nerve cell activity is the brain.
Brain activities and structures are associated with all human capacities including all sensations, thoughts, feelings, motives, actions (behaviors), and memories

ASSOCIATION AREAS

Areas of the cerebral cortex which have no sensory or motor function are known as the association cortex. They perform more complex functions such as language, memory, recognition, and problem solving. Damage to these areas can result in a loss of function, such as speech or the ability to recognize a friend.

HEMISPHERIC SPECIALIZATION

Brain functions are divided between the left and right halves (hemispheres).
The body's motor movement is controlled on opposite sides of the brain.
In most people, the left hemisphere controls language, and is superior in math, judging time and rhythm.
The right hemisphere is especially good at recognizing patterns, faces, and emotions.

SUBCORTEX

The areas that lie below the cerebral cortex are the subcortex. These areas control vital functions such as breathing, heart rate and swallowing. Unlike damage to the primary or association cortex, damage to the subcortical areas can be life threatening.

SYNAPTIC GAP

Neurons do not touch each other. A microscopic gap between neurons is the synapse. Messages pass across the synapse when neurotransmitters are released by the axon terminal.

RECEPTOR SITES

Areas on the surface of neurons and other cells that are sensitive to neurotransmitters or hormones are receptor sites.

Chapter 2:
The Brain, Biology, and Behavior

Practice Exam

1. Select the sequence indicating the normal flow of information in a nerve cell.
    a. soma, dendrites, axon terminals, axon
    b. dendrites, soma, axon, axon terminals
    c. axon, soma, dendrites, axon terminals
    d. dendrites, axon, myelin, axon terminals

2. The trigger point at which a neuron will "fire" is called the
    a. ion channel.
    b. resting potential.
    c. action potential.
    d. threshold.

3. The electrical discharge across a nerve cell membrane that generates a nerve impulse is called a(n)
    a. ion potential.
    b. neurotransmitter.
    c. action potential.
    d. dendrite signal.

4. Tiny areas on the surface of a cell that are sensitive to neurotransmitters are called
    a. axon terminals.
    b. somatic retention areas.
    c. dendritic retention areas.
    d. receptor sites.

5. The microscopic space between two neurons is called a(n)
    a. enkephalins.
    b. acetylcholine.
    c. catecholamine.
    d. synapse.

6. Which of the following cells will regenerate if damaged?
    a. a nerve cell in which the cell body dies
    b. a nerve cell in the brain
    c. a nerve cell wrapped in a neurilemma
    d. a nerve cell in the spinal cord

7.	When you see an attractive person sit down next to you on the bus, the mad pounding of your heart is under the influence of the
   a.	central nervous system.
   b.	diathesis nervous system.
   c.	autonomic nervous system.
   d.	somatic nervous system.

8.	_____ measures electrical activity of the brain by utilizing small disk-shaped metal plates that are placed on the person's scalp.
   a.	EEG
   b.	CT scan
   c.	MRI scan
   d.	PET

9.	The extent of the somatosensory area of the brain devoted to a particular part of the body is positively correlated with the body area's
   a.	size.
   b.	distance from the cortex.
   c.	sensitivity.
   d.	developmental significance.

10.	The human cerebral cortex
   a.	is comprised of white myelinated fibers.
   b.	looks like a peanut.
   c.	is composed of two hemispheres.
   d.	is covered with a smooth mantle of gray matter.

11.	Damage to which of the following would be most likely to cause visual problems?
   a.	the occipital lobe
   b.	the parietal lobe
   c.	the temporal lobes
   d.	the frontal lobes

12.	Children under age 2 who suffer left hemisphere damage can shift language processing to the right side of the brain but an adult probably could not do this because their brain has less
   a.	corticalization.
   b.	fluidity.
   c.	plasticity.
   d.	differentiation.

13.	The _____ connects the two halves of the brain.
   a.	corpus callosum
   b.	reticular formation
   c.	cerebellum
   d.	thalamus

14. The most accurate conclusion that can be drawn from research on the brain is that
    a.   normal people can be taught to use one hemisphere at a time.
    b.   ESB should be made illegal since it now can be used to control people against their will.
    c.   brain grafting can be used to reduce the effect of mental retardation.
    d.   the activities of both hemispheres of the brain combine to produce most behaviors.

15. The formation of memories depends on the
    a.   reticular formation.
    b.   corpus callosum.
    c.   hippocampus.
    d.   frontal lobe.

16. A person with brain damage who said "croth" for the word "cross" would most likely have damage to
    a.   the visual cortex.
    b.   Broca's area.
    c.   Wernicke's area.
    d.   the corpus callosum.

17. Controlling vital bodily functions is carried out primarily by
    a.   the hindbrain.
    b.   the midbrain.
    c.   the forebrain.
    d.   the occipital cortex.

18. Overactivity of the thyroid gland can lead to
    a.   tenseness, excitability, and nervousness.
    b.   inactivity, sleepiness, and slowness.
    c.   sleep disorders and disrupted body rhythms.
    d.   decreased salt levels.

19. Lateralization
    a.   refers to the specialization in the two sides of the brains.
    b.   is stronger in left-handed people than in right-handed people.
    c.   determines whether or not a person will be ambidextrous.
    d.   tends to make right-handed people smarter.

20. Among humans, about _____ percent are right-handed.
    a.   10
    b.   20
    c.   50
    d.   90

Try It!

Activity of the Brain

Answer the following short answer questions:

A. What part of the brain processes visual information?

B. What part of the brain processes what you hear?

C. What parts of the brain are involved when you hear something and look at it?

D. What parts of the brain will be "working" when you reach for something and pick it up?

E. What parts of the brain will be "working" when you hear someone ask you a question and you give the answer?

F. How could you informally evaluate someone's language skills?

Try It!

There are many articles in the media discussing the interrelationship between different foods and our hormones. For example, people are encouraged to take chromium to raise insulin, eat chocolate when our estrogen levels drop, or eat iodized salt to help our thyroid. Describe some of the media "blitzes" you have heard or read about or have personal experience with in the past few years.

Chapter 3 - Child Development

HUMAN DEVELOPMENT
Psychologists who study the progressive changes in behaviors and abilites from birth to death are known as <u>developmental psychologists</u>.

HEREDITY VERSUS ENVIRONMENT
Of particular interest in human development are the interactions of nature and nurture.

HEREDITY (NATURE)
An incredible number of personal features are set at conception. The transmission of physical and psychological characteristics from parents to offspring through genes influences temperament, susceptibility to diseases, potential cognitive abilities, and a great deal more.

ENVIRONMENT (NURTURE)
Environmental factors such as parental involvement, socio-economic situation, religion, personal experiences and many others are important to the developing human being. Environment refers to the sum of all external conditions affecting a person.

MATURATION
The physical growth of the body and nervous system is known as <u>maturation</u>. The orderly sequence of motor, cognitive, emotional, and language development is controlled by maturation.

You are a product of your genetic heritage and the environments in which you have lived.

NEWBORN CAPABILITIES
Newborn babies need the support of caregivers in order to survive. However they are born with certain capabilities that enable them to begin to interact with the world around them. Along with adaptive reflexes to root, suck and grasp, they can see, hear, smell, taste, and respond to pain and touch.

EMOTIONAL BONDING
Forming an emotional bond with a caregiver is a crucial event during infancy.

LANGUAGE
Learning language is a cornerstone of early intellectual development. The patterns of language development suggest a <u>biological predisposition</u> to acquire language, which is reinforced by learning. Children learn to control crying and babbling and proceed to single words and then telegraphic speech. Interaction between the child and parents is critical.

THINKING
Although a child's intellect is less abstract than an adult's, children come into the world prepared to acquire knowledge.

STAGE THEORY
Piaget's theory of child development through <u>stages</u> provides a valuable map of how thinking abilities unfold. Recent studies suggest that children are capable of thought well beyond that observed by Piaget.

SOCIOCULTURAL THEORY
Vygotsky's theory reminds us that a child's mind is shaped by interactions with more competent partners. These partners <u>scaffold</u> the child's progress.

PERSONAL DEVELOPMENT
does not end after adolescence
Periods of stability and transition
occur throughout adulthood.

DEVELOPMENTAL TASKS
Erik Erikson analyzed a series of psychological
challenges (psychosocial dilemmas) that occur
across the life-span. These range from gaining trust
in infancy, to living with integrity in old age.

DEPRIVATION and ENRICHMENT
All areas of child development are
affected by conditions of deprivation
(lack of normal stimulation, comfort, love)
or enrichment (a deliberately created
complex, stimulating, supportive
environment).
Parents (caregivers) play a significant
role in establishing conditions of
deprivation or enrichment.

TRUST
Learning to trust others and the world
comes from good parental care.

AUTONOMY
Developing self-control and independence
is essential to the developing sense of self
and self-esteem.

INITIATIVE
Learning to make plans and carry them out
is necessary for living in the adult world.

PARENTING & PARENTAL CARE
The quality of mothering and fathering (caregiving) that a child
receives is very important.
Proactive maternal involvement, how well a parent's temperament
matches the child's temperament (goodness of fit) and parent
responsiveness to the child all contribute to the child's development.
Primary caregivers may be the single greatest influence in a child's
environment.

INDUSTRY
Achieving goals and being recognized is
important to our sense of self-esteem.

IDENTITY
Forming a personal identity is a major task
of adolescence.

PARENTING STYLES
Studies show that caregiving
styles have a substantial impact
on emotional and intellectual
development. Three major
parental styles have been
identified:
Authoritarian
Permissive
Authoritative
Of the three, the most effective is
the authoritative.

CHILD DISCIPLINE
To be effective, child
discipline should:
stress responsibility;
involve mutual respect; and
be clear, consistent, and
humane.
Discipline should encourage a
child to seek positive
reinforcement.
Respectful communication
between parents and children
is essential.

INTIMACY
Establishing a circle of friends, family and a
partner.

GENERATIVITY
Being productive and developing an
interest in guiding the next generation.

INTEGRITY
Successful lives are based on happiness,
purpose, meaning, and integrity.

Chapter 3:
Child Development

Practice Exam

1. Temperament refers to
   a. psychological personality structures.
   b. physical foundations or core of personality.
   c. whether or not a child has a fever.
   d. an individual's current state of physical, emotional, and intellectual development.

2. Substances capable of causing birth defects are known as
   a. carcinogens.
   b. teratogens.
   c. chorionic villi.
   d. antigens.

3. Which of the following best represents the conclusions of the text regarding the relative effects of heredity and environment on development of individual characteristics?
   a. Heredity is the most influential, except for intelligence and personality.
   b. Environment is the most influential, although heredity plays a role.
   c. Neither heredity nor environment alone is very influential.
   d. Both heredity and environment exert powerful influences.

4. If you were to observe the development of psychomotor abilities in infants across cultures, you would find the most similarities in the
   a. ages at which abilities appear.
   b. child-rearing practices used to foster development.
   c. sequence in which abilities appear.
   d. relationship between intellectual and psychomotor development.

5. All basic human emotions appear before the age of
   a. 6 months.
   b. 1 year.
   c. 1 month.
   d. 2 years

6. Compared to mothers, fathers spend more time
   a. playing with the infant.
   b. feeding and care giving their infants.
   c. providing routine child care.
   d. that does not involve visual contact with the infant.

7. The normal order of language development in infancy is
   a. cooing, crying, babbling, telegraphic speech.
   b. crying, cooing, babbling, telegraphic speech.
   c. cooing, babbling, crying, telegraphic speech.
   d. telegraphic crying, cooing, babbling, elemental speech.

8. Dr. Jones is a psychologist who specializes in the psychology of language and language development. Dr. Jones would be referred to as a
   a. psycholinguist.
   b. paralanguage specialist.
   c. parapsychologist.
   d. preoperationalist.

9. The concreteness in young children's way of thinking is illustrated by their
   a. basing understanding of the world on that of their siblings.
   b. failure when very young to recognize the permanence of objects.
   c. ability to make rapid cognitive transformations.
   d. immediate use of the principle of conservation.

10. A child already knows the word "bird." When she sees a butterfly for the first time, she calls it a "bird" and is corrected by her mother. She learns the word "butterfly." This is an example of
    a. assimilation.
    b. accommodation.
    c. conservation.
    d. egocentrism.

11. The stages of life proposed by Erikson are distinct, as each pose
    a. failure to adjust to one's new surroundings.
    b. a specific crisis or dilemma that must be resolved.
    c. a major source of psychosomatic disorder.
    d. a stage of physiological development.

12. According to Erikson, a child entering adolescence can expect major developmental task demands to center around the need to
    a. develop trust in others.
    b. achieve intimacy with another.
    c. acquire personal autonomy.
    d. develop a sense of one's self.

13. Which method of dealing with the problem of child abuse is considered to be most effective in the long run?
    a. placing abused children in foster homes
    b. self-help groups such as Parents Anonymous
    c. changing our attitudes toward physical punishment
    d. incarcerating the parents

14. Identification with peer groups
    a. decreases during adolescence.
    b. gives an adolescent a measure of security and a sense of identity.
    c. reduces self-esteem and self-worth.
    d. seems to always lead to incredibly destructive behaviors.

15. Kohlberg identified the three levels of moral development as the
    a. preconventional, conventional, and postconventional.
    b. conditional, unconditional, and postconditional.
    c. self-interested, social, and personal.
    d. premoral, conventional, and postethical.

16. Life satisfaction in old age seems to depend upon
    a. maintaining physically demanding occupational roles.
    b. continued performance in roles considered important by society.
    c. the system of social support maintained for people as they disengage from all activities.
    d. spending time doing things that people find meaningful.

17. Aging is gradual with peak functioning occurring at 25 or 30.
    a. Thereafter gradual declines continue in physical and sensory functions.
    b. Thereafter rapid declines occur.
    c. Thereafter there is no decline.
    d. Sensory enhancement is common following the age of 40.

18. Which of the following is a myth about aging?
    a. Most older individuals are the best drivers on the road.
    b. Most of the elderly show signs of senility and mental decay.
    c. The elderly who live alone are typically "social butterflies."
    d. Older individuals are just as sexually active as when they were 30.

19. Cultural influences on morality show that people from Eastern cultures are more likely to put _____ welfare over individual welfare.
    a. their
    b. problem solving
    c. group
    d. none of these

20. Conforming to the expectations of others or to socially accepted rules and values describes a person at the _____ level of morality.
    a. obedience
    b. concrete
    c. postconventional
    d. conventional

Try It!
Broadening Our Cultural Horizons

A. **Collect information on the Israeli kibbutz system of child-rearing.** What are the advantages and disadvantages of this system?

B. **Different cultures "see" children in different ways.** How do you view children? Circle the number that is closest to your views:

I see children (age 5 to 12) as:

big babies	1	2	3	4	5	*little adults*
helpless	1	2	3	4	5	*responsible*
dependent	1	2	3	4	5	*independent*
fragile	1	2	3	4	5	*sturdy*
not smart	1	2	3	4	5	*very smart*
self-centered	1	2	3	4	5	*other-directed*

Share your views with others in class. In what ways are your views similar and different?

C. **Often step-families blend two very different "cultures" in terms of rules and expectations of behavior.** What would you suggest that step-families do to minimize the culture shock as the families merge?

D. **Research suggests that certain facial expressions are universally expressed.** What does this suggest about the possibility of effective international communication?

E. **If you are bilingual, discuss the advantages and disadvantages you have encountered with your group members.** If any of your classmates are visiting from other countries, or if they are recent immigrants, ask them to tell you how child-rearing practices are different in their home culture.

F. **Investigate the place that children occupy in a family setting in various cultures.** Compare the findings with the way children are raised in our culture.

Try It!

Consider the following questions and provide answers based on your own experience.

A. Do you know any parents who have young children and who are authoritarian, permissive, or authoritative?

B. What are their children like?

C. What do you think are the best ways to discipline children?

D. How would your approach to discipline be classified based on information from the text? What are its advantages and disadvantages?

Try It!

Think about friends of yours in school over the years, and how different types of learning disorders have affected your friends' achievement in school. Suggest how difficulties such as attention deficit disorder, reading disabilities, speech impediments such as stuttering, etc., also affected their social and emotional development.

Try It!
Erikson's Ages and Stages

This is an assignment to help you understand Erik Erikson's eight stages of psychosocial development. Review the descriptions of behaviors appropriate to each of the stages.

Select three people of different ages whom you know well. One of them should be yourself. Try to identify which of Erikson's stages best describes the person's overall behavior. Don't be influenced by the person's age. People don't always "act their age!" You need to explain your decision in each case.

Subject #1   Age_____   Stage_____

Behaviors:

Reasons:

Subject #2   Age_____   Stage_____

Behaviors:

Reasons:

Subject #3   Age_____   Stage_____

Behaviors:

Reasons:

Chapter 4 - Sensation and Perception

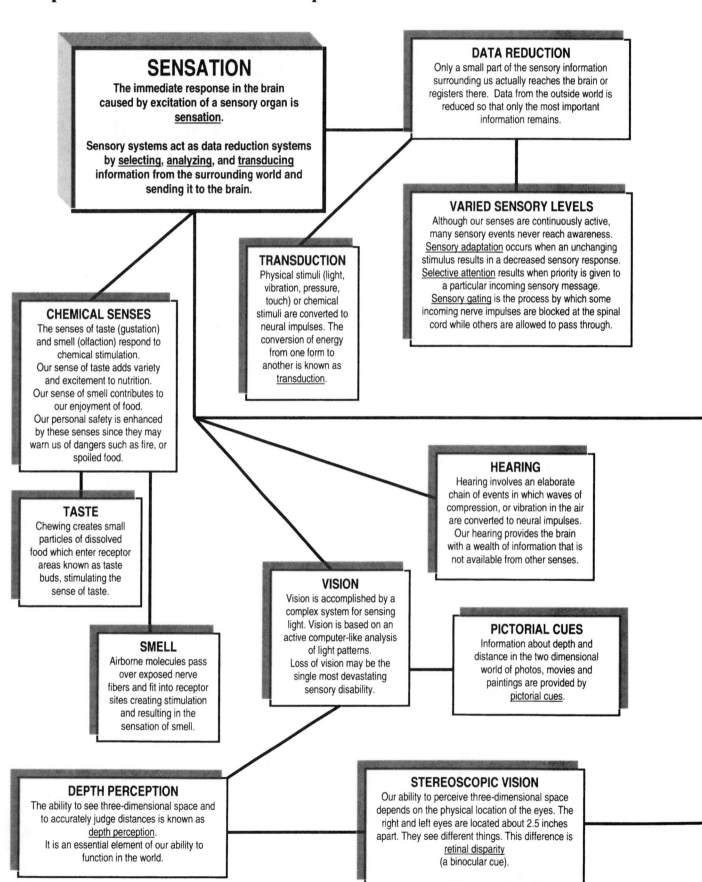

SENSATION
The immediate response in the brain caused by excitation of a sensory organ is <u>sensation</u>.

Sensory systems act as data reduction systems by <u>selecting</u>, <u>analyzing</u>, and <u>transducing</u> information from the surrounding world and sending it to the brain.

DATA REDUCTION
Only a small part of the sensory information surrounding us actually reaches the brain or registers there. Data from the outside world is reduced so that only the most important information remains.

VARIED SENSORY LEVELS
Although our senses are continuously active, many sensory events never reach awareness. <u>Sensory adaptation</u> occurs when an unchanging stimulus results in a decreased sensory response. <u>Selective attention</u> results when priority is given to a particular incoming sensory message. <u>Sensory gating</u> is the process by which some incoming nerve impulses are blocked at the spinal cord while others are allowed to pass through.

TRANSDUCTION
Physical stimuli (light, vibration, pressure, touch) or chemical stimuli are converted to neural impulses. The conversion of energy from one form to another is known as <u>transduction</u>.

CHEMICAL SENSES
The senses of taste (gustation) and smell (olfaction) respond to chemical stimulation.
Our sense of taste adds variety and excitement to nutrition.
Our sense of smell contributes to our enjoyment of food.
Our personal safety is enhanced by these senses since they may warn us of dangers such as fire, or spoiled food.

TASTE
Chewing creates small particles of dissolved food which enter receptor areas known as taste buds, stimulating the sense of taste.

SMELL
Airborne molecules pass over exposed nerve fibers and fit into receptor sites creating stimulation and resulting in the sensation of smell.

HEARING
Hearing involves an elaborate chain of events in which waves of compression, or vibration in the air are converted to neural impulses. Our hearing provides the brain with a wealth of information that is not available from other senses.

VISION
Vision is accomplished by a complex system for sensing light. Vision is based on an active computer-like analysis of light patterns.
Loss of vision may be the single most devastating sensory disability.

PICTORIAL CUES
Information about depth and distance in the two dimensional world of photos, movies and paintings are provided by <u>pictorial cues</u>.

DEPTH PERCEPTION
The ability to see three-dimensional space and to accurately judge distances is known as <u>depth perception</u>.
It is an essential element of our ability to function in the world.

STEREOSCOPIC VISION
Our ability to perceive three-dimensional space depends on the physical location of the eyes. The right and left eyes are located about 2.5 inches apart. They see different things. This difference is <u>retinal disparity</u> (a binocular cue).

PERCEPTION

The active process of <u>assembling</u> sensations into <u>meaningful patterns</u> that represent external events is <u>perception</u>.

PERCEPTUAL GROUPINGS

We unconsciously use the Gestalt principles to organize sensations into meaningful patterns.

<u>Figure-ground</u>: the simplest form of organization prompts one object to stand out from another, plainer background. The writing on this paper is <u>figure</u> while the paper itself is <u>ground</u>.

<u>Nearness</u>: stimuli that are near each other tend to be grouped together.

<u>Similarity</u>: stimuli that are similar in size, shape, color or form tend to be grouped together.

<u>Continuity</u>: complex stimuli tend to be perceived in the simplest form.

<u>Closure</u>: incomplete figures tend to be completed by our perceptions.

<u>Contiguity</u>: nearness in time and space often results in a perception that one thing has *caused* another.

<u>Common region</u>: stimuli found within a common area tend to be perceived as a group, regardless of their similarities to one another.

PERCEPTUAL CONSTANCIES

Our vision would be unstable and would seem distorted and erratic if not for the perceptual constancies.

<u>Size constancy</u>: the perceived size of objects remains the same even though the retinal image has changed.

<u>Shape constancy</u>: the perceived shape of an object remains the same in spite of changes in the retinal image.

<u>Brightness constancy</u>: so long as the same proportion of light illuminates objects, their brightness will remain constant.

PERCEPTUAL INFLUENCES

Our experiences are perceptual re-constructions (mental models of external events). Private perceptual experiences do not always accurately represent external events. Our personal needs, expectations, attitudes, beliefs, learning, and values influence our perceptions of events.

PERCEPTUAL ACCURACY

The accuracy and objectivity of perceptions can be improved through conscious effort and an awareness of factors that contribute to erroneous perceptions.

SOMESTHETIC SENSES

Sensations that are produced by the skin, muscles, joints, viscera, and organs of balance are known as the somesthetic senses.

They are important to us because they provide us with information vital to our survival.

VESTIBULAR SENSES

Our sense of balance, gravity and acceleration are the vestibular senses. Receptors in the inner ear provide these sensations.

SKIN

Our skin receptors provide us with at least five different sensations: <u>light touch</u>, <u>pressure</u>, <u>pain</u>, <u>cold</u>, and <u>warmth</u>.

KINESTHETIC SENSES

The kinesthetic senses provide us with an awareness of <u>body position and movement</u> through receptors in muscles and joints.

Knowing where our body parts are located in space is important to us as we sit, walk, close the car door and a variety of other activities.

EXTRA SENSORY PERCEPTION (ESP)

The purported ability to perceive events in ways that cannot be explained by known sensory capacities is known as <u>extrasensory perception</u>.

<u>Inconsistent statistics</u> and the <u>inability to replicate results</u> under similar circumstances stand in the way of scientific acceptance of extrasensory perception.

MUSCULAR CUES

The body itself provides cues concerning depth and distance.

Changes in the shape of the lens of the eye are referred to as <u>accommodation</u>.

The simultaneous turning in of the eye controlled by muscles is known as <u>convergence</u> (a binocular cue).

Chapter 4:
Sensation and Perception

Practice Exam
1.   Visual perception is ultimately a function of the
       a.   muscular movements of the eye.
       b.   neural activity of the rods and cones.
       c.   particular pathways over which neural impulses travel.
       d.   neural activity in the brain.

2.   The part of the eye that focuses the image is called the
       a.   lens.
       b.   retina.
       c.   iris.
       d.   pupil.

3.   The amount of light entering the eye is regulated by the
       a.   lens.
       b.   cornea.
       c.   iris.
       d.   diaphragm.

4.   The cones of the retina
       a.   are densely packed in the periphery of the retina.
       b.   are specialized for color sensations.
       c.   function best in dim light conditions.
       d.   lack the ability to respond to fine detail.

5.   Which theory of color vision holds that there are three types of cones that respond
      to red, green, and blue (respectively)?
       a.   opponent-process theory
       b.   trichromatic theory
       c.   three-opponent theory
       d.   stage primary theory

6.   Which one of the following sequences is the correct one for audition?
       a.   ear drum, cochlea, hair cells, ossicles
       b.   ossicles, ear drum, cochlea, hair cells
       c.   hair cells, ossicles, ear drum, cochlea
       d.   ear drum, ossicles, cochlea, hair cells

7.   Olfaction and gustation are considered
       a.   chemical senses.
       b.   vestibular senses.
       c.   unrelated to each other.
       d.   of little importance in mammals.

8. The vestibular sense helps keep us from
   a. eating too much.
   b. starving to death.
   c. being blinded by the sun.
   d. falling over.

9. Which of the following best characterizes the process of perception?
   a. a passive activity by which information about the real world is transmitted to the brain by sense organs
   b. the exact recording of the kind and quality of energy present in the environment
   c. an automatic process by which a stream of incoming stimulation triggers images stored in the brain
   d. an active process by which sensory input is selected, organized, and integrated

10. Closure, nearness, similarity, and continuation are categories of
    a. perceptual (Gestalt) organization.
    b. cognitive style.
    c. cognitive organization.
    d. perceptual integration.

11. The ability to see three-dimensional space and to accurately judge distances is called
    a. size constancy.
    b. shape constancy.
    c. depth perception.
    d. perceptual organization.

12. A person living in the desert calls a 60 degree day "cold" whereas one living in Alaska calls it "warm." Their perceptions differ because of
    a. attention shifts.
    b. their frame of reference.
    c. temperature parallax.
    d. perceptual constancy.

13. The depth cue in which there is an apparent convergence of parallel lines is called
    a. overlap.
    b. retinal disparity.
    c. linear perspective.
    d. accommodation.

14. Pictorial cues for depth are
    a. monocular.
    b. binocular.
    c. bodily.
    d. stereoscopic.

15. The Müller-Lyer illusion
    a. does not exist in cultures with extensive experience with architural design.
    b. is based upon figure-ground relationships.
    c. is seldom experienced by Zulus.
    d. is only present with arrows and lines less that one foot in length.

16. The analysis of information starting with features and building into a complete perception is known as
    a. perceptual expectancy.
    b. top-down processing.
    c. bottom-up processing.
    d. Gregory's phenomenon.

17. The text suggests that enhanced perceptual accuracy would be achieved through
    a. forming perceptual habits.
    b. using divided attention principles.
    c. being aware of motives and expectations that can influence your perceptions.
    d. quitting the use of our hard-wired concepts and schemas.

18. The underlying mechanism for perceptual expectancies is
    a. a misleading perception that distorts or misjudges a stimulus.
    b. top-down processing.
    c. the organization of perception by beginning with low-level features.
    d. bottom-up processing.

19. The purported ability to predict future events is called
    a. clairvoyance.
    b. precognition.
    c. psychokinesis.
    d. telepathy.

20. Many psychologists doubt the existence of psi abilities because
    a. they have not experienced it themselves.
    b. few persons claim to have such abilities.
    c. there are few systematic attempts to investigate such phenomena.
    d. improved methodology often leads to fewer positive results.

Try It!

Develop a series of analogies for each of the senses: Which sense is most like a video? A CD? A TV? A computer? A battery-operated child's toy? A balloon? A musical instrument? A tea pot? In what important ways are the senses different in each case?

Try It!

Do various cultures emphasize different sensory channels to a greater or lesser degree? For example, do some cultures place more emphasis on touch, taste, or smell than North Americans do? What does the American preoccupation with television tell us about our culture? The French reputation for cooking? The Italian tendency to touch a person when talking to her or him?

Try It!

Various cultures have different approaches to pain management. Some groups suggest that pain should be ignored; others acknowledge pain but suggest specific ways to deal with it. What did the "mini-culture" of your family suggest? If you suddenly feel pain in your chest, what has your culture taught you to do? Are these behaviors adaptive or maladaptive?

Try It!

For a simple illustration of convergence, focus on a distant point and then bring a finger up into the line of sight. The finger will appear "transparent" because the line of sight is nearly parallel. Now look directly at the finger, it will once again become "solid" (convergence). A variation on this (which also illustrates retinal disparity and fusion) involves again fixating on a distant point. This time the tips of the index fingers of both hands should be brought together in the line of sight, about twelve inches from the eyes. You should see a small "sausage" forming and disappearing between their fingertips as the two retinal images overlap.

Try It!

Because perceptions are reconstructions or models of external events we should all engage in more frequent reality testing. Can you think of a recent event when a little reality testing would have saved you from misjudging a situation?

Chapter 5 - States of Consciousness

CONSCIOUSNESS
To be conscious means to be aware. Consciousness consists of all the sensations, perceptions, memories, and feelings we are aware of at any instant.

WAKING CONSCIOUSNESS
Waking consciousness is a state of clear, organized, alertness in which we perceive times, places, and events as real, meaningful, and familiar.

ALTERED STATES
During an altered state of consciousness (ASC), changes occur in the quality and pattern of mental activity typically with distinct shifts in perceptions, emotions, memory time sense, thinking, feelings of self-control, and suggestibility.

DRUG ALTERED CONSIOUSNESS
The surest way to alter human consciousness is to administer a psychoactive drug (a substance which can alter attention, memory, judgement, time sense, self-control, mood, or perception.

PSYCHOACTIVE DRUGS
Substances capable of altering attention, memory, judgement, time sense, self-control, mood, or perception are considered to be psychoactive drugs.
Physical dependence (addiction) may result from extended use.
Drug tolerance (a reduced response to the drug) often accompanies addiction.
Psychological dependence develops when an individual feels that a drug is necessary to maintain feelings of comfort or well-being.

DEPRESSANT or STIMULANT
Most psychoactive drugs can be placed on a scale ranging from stimulation to depression. A substance that increases activity in the body and nervous system is a stimulant.
A substance that decreases activity in the body and nervous system is a depressant.

DOWNERS
Drugs such as alcohol, tranquilizers and sedatives inhibit brain function.
Barbiturates are sedatives that in high doses can cause severe mental confusion. Overdoes can cause coma or death.
Tranquilizers lower anxiety and reduce tension. Addiction is a strong possibility.
Alcohol, contrary to popular belief, is not a stimulant. Continued use of large amounts cause ever-greater impairment of the brain.

UPPERS
Stimulant drugs excite the brain, but severe risks accompany their use.
Amphetamines rapidly produce a drug tolerance; speed up the use of bodily resources; and in come cases, have caused permanent brain damage.
Cocaine can cause convulsions, heart attacks, or strokes.
Caffeine use may result in insomnia, irritability, appetite loss and elevated body temperature.
Nicotine from smoking is undeniably related to cancers.

HALLUCINOGENS
Hallucinogens are substances which alter or distort sensory impressions.
LSD is possibly the best known hallucinogen. In combination with other drugs it may cause extreme agitation and violence.
Marijuana's effects have been the center of debate. Recent research confirms some forms of brain damage, immune system problems, and a variety of other difficulties associated with use of marijuana.

HYPNOSIS

Hypnotists use many different methods to induce an altered state of consciousness characterized by narrowed attention and an increased openness to suggestion.
All techniques encourage focused attention, inducement to relax, and heightened imagination.

MEDITATION

Meditation refers to mental exercises that are used to alter consciousness.
Many claims have been made regarding the benefits of meditation. Many such claims appear to be overstated. Meditation does reliably bring about the relaxation response.

SLEEP DISTURBANCES

Sleep disorders
are serious health problems that should be corrected when they persist. Thousands of people are treated each year.
Insomnia is a difficulty in getting to sleep or staying asleep. Behavioral techniques and lifestyle changes are preferred methods of treatment.
Sleepwalking and sleeptalking occur during NREM sleep.
Sleep apnea (interrupted breathing) is a source of insomnia and daytime sleepiness. It may be one cause of sudden infant death syndrome (SIDS).

SLEEP

Sleep is the most common Altered State of Consciousness (ASC).
Sleep is necessary for survival of the individual.
Mental illness or death may result from insufficient sleep.

REM & Non-REM SLEEP

Sleep occurs in two basic states:
Rapid Eye Movement (REM) sleep helps us form memories and it contributes to general mental effectiveness. REM sleep is generally associated with dreaming.
Non-REM sleep is generally free of dreams.

MEANING IN DREAMS?

Whether dreams have deeper, symbolic meaning is still debated. Many theorists question Freud's view of dreams. The activation-synthesis model portrays dreaming as a physiological process.

Effects of Sleep Loss

Moderate sleep loss affects vigilance and performance.
Sleep deprivation psychosis may result from extended sleep loss.
Many highway accidents may be a result of microsleeps.

FOUR STAGES OF SLEEP

Sleep occurs in four stages ranging from shallow to deep. Each stage is marked by different brain wave patterns.

DREAMS & PERSONAL UNDERSTANDING

Each dream has several possible meanings or levels of meaning.
Remembering and recording your dream upon awakening is important.
Probing the dream content for who the characters were; what happened; where and when the dream occurred; and who is responsible for actions in the dream can lead to understanding the meaning of the dream.
A technique known as lucid dreaming can be learned to assist in understanding dreams.

Chapter 5:
States of Consciousness

Practice Exam

1. Consciousness
   a. has been described as an ever-changing flow of awareness.
   b. includes only perceptions from the internal world.
   c. is most often unorganized.
   d. is outside of an individual's direct control.

2. To be conscious means to be _____ .
   a. dreaming
   b. aware
   c. dynamic
   d. in REM

3. When a person is shut off from the world such that he or she cannot even tell what time it is by light or dark, their sleep-waking cycle
   a. stays at about 24 hours.
   b. shortens to an average of about 20 hours.
   c. lengthens to an average of about 25 hours.
   d. becomes completely disrupted.

4. How many hours of sleep do the majority of adults get per night?
   a. five hours
   b. seven to eight hours
   c. ten hours
   d. twelve hours

5. Which of the following statements about sleep is FALSE?
   a. Sleep is a state of unconsciousness caused by the accumulation of chemicals in the blood.
   b. During sleep, individuals can solve problems, respond to stimuli in the environment, and perform simple tasks.
   c. Sleep is essential to normal psychological functioning and life.
   d. Most symptoms of sleep deprivation can be alleviated by a single night's sleep.

6. Short bursts of brain activity in Stage 2 sleep are called
   a. delta waves.
   b. recurrent beta waves.
   c. sleep spindles.
   d. cortical waves.

7.   Which of the following sleep phenomena could be detected without the aid of an EEG machine?
       a.   Stage 2 sleep
       b.   REM sleep
       c.   Stage 3 sleep
       d.   sleep spindles

8.   Which statement about REM sleep is TRUE?
       a.   REM sleep accounts for 80 percent of our sleep time.
       b.   Dreams occur only in REM sleep.
       c.   REM sleep periods get longer as the night's sleep progresses.
       d.   Birds, mammals, and reptiles all show REM sleep.

9.   When a person periodically stops breathing during sleep, we say they have
       a.   REM rebound effect.
       b.   sleep apnea.
       c.   narcolepsy.
       d.   somnambulism.

10.   The theory that relates dream content to motor commands in the brain, which are made but not carried out during sleep, is called the _____ theory.
       a.   psychodynamic
       b.   wish fulfillment
       c.   activation-synthesis
       d.   hypnosis

11.   _____ is a factor common to all hypnotic techniques.
       a.   Repetitively saying "sleep, sleep"
       b.   Increasing heart rate and blood pressure
       c.   Letting go and accepting suggestions
       d.   Synthesizing wish fulfillment

12.   Lapses in awareness, bizarre sensations, and perceptual distortions are all responses associated with
       a.   perceptual enhancement.
       b.   perceptual fatigue.
       c.   ensory deprivation.
       d.   selective perception.

13.   Which of the following is a goal of the therapeutic use of meditation?
       a.   decompression of the ventricular system
       b.   experiencing relaxation and reducing stress
       c.   producing delusions
       d.   producing hallucinations

14. Abuse of which of the following is the biggest drug problem in the United States?
    a. cocaine
    b. alcohol
    c. heroin
    d. barbiturates

15. Which of the following statement regarding marijuana is FALSE?
    a. Its immediate effects are euphoria, altered time sense, and impaired immediate memory.
    b. Experts agree that it has little effect on driving performance.
    c. Extreme dosages can cause feelings of unreality and visual distortions.
    d. Marijuana's potential for abuse lies primarily in the realm of psychological dependence, not addiction.

16. Smoking
    a. is responsible for 97% of lung cancer deaths in men.
    b. is responsible for 74% of lung cancer deaths in women.
    c. is responsible for a 4 to 6 times higher risk of developing oral cancer (using smokeless tobacco).
    d. research regarding its link to cancer, show all of these are true.

17. Which of the following drugs is physically addictive?
    a. morphine
    b. cocaine
    c. heroin
    d. all of these

18. According to Freud, the dream process in which important emotions are redirected toward safe or seemingly unimportant images is
    a. secondary elaboration.
    b. condensation.
    c. displacement.
    d. symbolization.

19. The text outlines a procedure for using dreams in problem solving that involves which of the following?
    a. Employ daydreams by deliberately "withdrawing" into fantasy during the day.
    b. Use prescription medication to increase your likelihood of dreaming.
    c. Concentrate on the problem just before going to bed and then use dream "catching" techniques.
    d. Increase your time spent in sleep thus directly increasing the time for dreams to occur.

20. A person who "wakes" within a dream and becomes aware that he/she is dreaming is
    a. experiencing a night terror.
    b. having a lucid dream.
    c. sleeptalking.
    d. awake.

Try It!
The members of many cultures seek altered states of consciousness as pathways to enlightenment and personal power. What are the predominant means of altering consciousness in our culture? Are any of them potential pathways for personal growth?

Try It!
Sleep Patterns
Identify which problems do you, your friends, or relatives have. For example,
     a. do they sleep much below or much more than average;
     b. have they been deprived of sleep for long periods;
     c. have they done shift work or have maintained unusual sleep/working cycles;
     d. do they have a relative or acquaintance who has had sleep disturbances such as somnambulism, night terrors, narcolepsy, sleep apnea, or insomnia.

Try It!
Sleep and Dreams
While many express great interest in the topic of sleep and dreams, it is a subject about which many have misconceptions. J. Palladino and B. Carducci have developed *A Sleep and Dream Information Questionnaire* designed to assess student awareness of current findings in sleep and dream research. This questionnaire can provide an interesting and informative way to introduce yourself to this material. Copies of the questionnaire, an appendix entitled "Explanation of Items Comprising the Sleep and Dream Information Questionnaire," and reprints are available from Joseph Palladino, Department of Psychology, Indiana State University at Evansville. For more information see J. J. Palladino and B. J. Carducci, "Students' Knowledge of Sleep and Dreams," *Teaching of Psychology*, Vol. II (3), October 1984.

Try It!

<u>Dreaming: Data Sheet</u>

Record on this sheet the answers to the following questions about your dreams. Write your responses as soon as you awake in the morning.

A.   What dream(s) did you have last night? What happened? What people or animals were present?

B.   What were you doing or thinking about immediately before going to bed?

C.   What significant experiences did you have yesterday or in the last few days?

D.   Are you anticipating any important events today or in the next few days? What are they?

Try It!
Drug Questionnaire

A. What role do drugs play in American culture? In your life?

B. To what extent is your use of drugs (including non-prescription drugs) an expression of cultural patterns and values?

C. What cultural values do you think would increase the likelihood of drug use or abuse?

D. What similarities would you guess would exist among drug abusers in various cultures, regardless of their race, gender, or ethnic background?

Chapter 6 - Conditioning and Learning

REINFORCEMENT

Reinforcement refers to any event that increases the probability that a response will occur again.
Responses are any identifiable behavior. They may be observable or they may be hidden from direct viewing (as in increased heartbeat, or an emotional feeling).
Responses that are followed by reinforcement become more frequent.

LEARNING

Learning is a relatively permanent change in behavior due to experience. Temporary changes in behavior due to motivation, drugs, injury or disease are not learning.

SCHEDULES OF REINFORCEMENT

Schedules of reinforcement reflect which responses will be reinforced.
Continuous reinforcement requires that each response be reinforced.
Partial reinforcement occurs when only some responses are reinforced.
Responses acquired by a partial reinforcement schedule are resistant to becoming extinct (weakening or disappearing).
The number of times a response is reinforced (ratio) and the time between reinforcements (interval) determine the more common partial schedules of reinforcement.

CLASSICAL CONDITIONING

Classical conditioning is a fundamental type of learning in which reflex responses are associated with new stimuli.
In this form of learning, the responses are reflexive (involuntary responses).

UNCONDITIONED STIMULUS (US)

A stimulus that reliably provokes an involuntary response (typically physiological and/or emotional) is an Unconditioned Stimulus.

Example: Meat powder

NEUTRAL STIMULI (NS)

A neutral stimulus is one that does not cause a response. It is repeatedly paired with an Unconditioned Stimulus.

Example: Bell

UNCONDITIONED RESPONSE (UR)

The involuntary response to an unconditioned stimulus is an unconditioned response (UR).

Example: Salivation

CONDITIONED STIMULUS (CS)

By association, the neutral stimulus also begins to elicit a response. The neutral stimulus is no longer neutral. It has become a conditioned stimulus (CS).

The bell is now a CS.

EMOTIONS & CONDITIONING

Conditioning affects us in various ways. Phobias are fears that persist when no realistic danger exists. Phobias often begin with conditioned emotional responses (CERs).

ONE MORE EXAMPLE: Pain is a US. Elevation of the autonomic nervous system (Chap. 2) in response to pain is a UR. A raised hand begins as an NS. However, if pain is preceded by the sight of the raised hand, the hand becomes a CS and the body starts to elevate the ANS before the pain is actually experienced.

CONDITIONED RESPONSE

A learned response elicited by a conditioned stimulus.

Salivating in response to the bell, before the meat powder is applied.

ANTECEDENTS & CONSEQUENCES

Events that precede a response are <u>antecedents</u>.
Effects that follow a response are <u>consequences</u>.
Consequences are neither "good" nor "bad". Rather, they are simply the events that follow a behavior.

CONDITIONING & PRACTICAL PROBLEMS

Learning principles may be used to manage one's own behavior or the behavior of others.
Operant learning can be used to manage the discipline of children.
Behavioral self-management techniques enable a person to reinforce behaviors they want to increase and eliminate undesirable behaviors.

OBSERVATIONAL LEARNING (MODELING)

We learn by observing and imitating the actions of others. From others we can learn new responses; how to carry out or avoid previously learned responses; and learn general rules that can be applied in a variety of situations. For observational learning to occur:
1. We must <u>pay attention</u> to the model.
2. We must <u>be able</u> to reproduce the model's behavior.
Whether a behavior is actually imitated will be determined by whether the model was reinforced or punished.

OPERANT CONDITIONING

(voluntary behaviors)
In this form of learning the consequences of behavior determine if the behavior will be repeated voluntarily.

COGNITIVE LEARNING

Cognitive learning involves acquiring higher level information, rather than just linking stimuli and responses. Cognitive learning extends to the use of memory, thinking, problem solving, and use of language.
<u>Cognitive maps</u> are internal representations of relationships between pieces of information (such as where you are and where you want to be in a city, or how one element of psychology relates to another). *These visual guides are based on the concept of cognitive mapping.*
<u>Latent learning</u> occurs without any obvious reinforcement and remains hidden until reinforcement is provided.
<u>Discovery learning</u> occurs when people discover facts and principles on their own through insight and understanding.

POSITIVE REINFORCEMENT

Positive Reinforcement occurs when a behavior is followed by a positive event (a reinforcer that is desired by the one performing the behavior).
Positive reinforcement <u>increases</u> the probability that the behavior will be repeated.

NEGATIVE REINFORCEMENT

Negative reinforcement is NOT the same as punishment.
Negative reinforcement occurs when a behavior ends an aversive stimulus or restores a response cost.
Negative reinforcement <u>increases</u> the probability that a behavior will be repeated.

NON – REINFORCEMENT

When no reinforcement occurs following a behavior, the probability of the behavior being repeated is <u>decreased</u>.

PUNISHMENT

Punishment takes <u>two forms</u>.
<u>Aversive stimulus</u> punishment occurs when a physically or psychologically aversive event (such as a spanking, or a parent's lecture) follows the behavior.
<u>Response cost</u> punishment occurs when a positive circumstance is taken away (such as when a child loses T.V. privileges or is "grounded").
Punishment <u>decreases</u> the probability that a behavior will be repeated.

Chapter 6:
Conditioning and Learning

Practice Exam

1. Which of the following plays a major role in learned behavior?
    a. fatigue
    b. maturation
    c. affect
    d. reinforcement

2. In classical conditioning, learning is evident when a
    a. stimulus automatically produces a response without a prior history of experience.
    b. stimulus which did not initially produce a response now elicits that response.
    c. spontaneously emitted response increases in frequency as a result of its consequences.
    d. subject repeats an action he or she has observed in another and is praised for it.

3. In Pavlov's experiments with dogs, the conditioned response was the
    a. food.
    b. bell.
    c. salivation to the food.
    d. salivation to the bell.

4. A child is frightened by a loud noise while playing with a cat. If the child learns to fear the cat, it can be said that the cat was
    a. the UR.
    b. a generalization gradient.
    c. the US.
    d. a CS.

5. The process of weakening learned conditioned responses by removing reinforcement is called
    a. spontaneous recovery.
    b. expiration.
    c. unconditioning.
    d. extinction.

6. The technique of using desensitization involves
    a. flooding the person with images of the feared stimulus.
    b. gradually exposing the person to the feared stimulus.
    c. gradually exposing the person to the feared stimulus only when they are fully relaxed.
    d. systematically increasing the stimulus intensity up to the breaking point.

7. An object or event that increases the probability of a response is an operant
   a. reward.
   b. incentive.
   c. reinforcer.
   d. discriminator.

8. The process through which a response is taught by rewarding successive approximations to the final desired response is
   a. extinction.
   b. fading.
   c. shaping.
   d. secondary reinforcement.

9. Your niece has a temper tantrum in the store when she is shopping. If you buy her a toy you are
   a. being practical.
   b. being kind.
   c. encouraging more tantrums.
   d. discouraging more destructive behaviors.

10. For rats in a Skinner box, if the delay between bar pressing and receiving food is greater than about 90 seconds,
    a. very little learning occurs.
    b. learning is relatively unaffected.
    c. learning increases.
    d. no learning occurs.

11. Superstitious behavior
    a. is based upon an apparent connection between a response and a reward.
    b. is necessary to produce reinforcement.
    c. is observed only in people.
    d. are learned patterns that consistently predict future events.

12. Negative reinforcement occurs when a response
    a. leads to a desirable consequence.
    b. leads to the removal of an unpleasant event.
    c. leads to an undesirable consequence.
    d. is ignored.

13. When a basketball coach uses videotaped replays to show his team both their good and poor shot selection, the coach is using
    a. CAI.
    b. feedback.
    c. punishment.
    d. two-factor learning.

14. All interval schedules of reinforcement are
    a.   more resistant to generalization.
    b.   related to the passage of time.
    c.   less resistant to extinction.
    d.   better for generating operant responses.

15. Each time the owner of an aquarium turns on the aquarium light, the fish gather in the corner in which he routinely places food. Because he always turns the light on before feeding the fish, their actions demonstrate
    a.   spontaneous recovery.
    b.   extinction.
    c.   stimulus control.
    d.   resistance to extinction.

16. Using punishment can be "habit forming" because putting a stop to someone else's irritating behavior can
    a.   positively reinforce the person who applies the punishment.
    b.   negatively reinforce the person who applies the punishment.
    c.   encourage the person to use punishment less often in the future.
    d.   lead to the liberal use of positive reinforcers.

17. You have never played baseball before, but you know most of the rules from watching TV. This illustrates
    a.   classical conditioning.
    b.   instrumental conditioning.
    c.   stimulus generalization.
    d.   latent learning.

18. Research suggests that children will imitate
    a.   what a parent says he or she should do.
    b.   whom a parent designates as a model.
    c.   what a parent does.
    d.   what a parent wishes he or she would do.

19. The most important role of television in the modeling of aggressive behavior may be that TV violence
    a.   is seen as an acceptable way for both villains and heroes to act.
    b.   arouses basic human instincts for aggression.
    c.   leads to unconscious desires for aggression and power.
    d.   provides an acceptable outlet for otherwise destructive behaviors.

20. Which of the following is an example of a strategy of self-regulated learning?
    a.   rewarding yourself on a variable interval schedule
    b.   implementing strategies for programmed responses
    c.   planning a learning strategy
    d.   waiting until the end to monitor success or failure

Try It!

Give these questions a shot! Why does your:
a. dog drool when you open the can of food before the food is given to him?
b. friend flinch when you tickle him or her?
c. little sister tremble at the sound of a dentist's drill?
d. fellow student begin blushing before he or she is called on to give a speech?
e. stomach churn when the teacher says, "Take out a piece of paper and put your name at the top"?

Try It!

Describe superstitious behaviors you have observed in televised sporting events.
a. Is it possible that these behaviors actually are reinforcers?
b. What makes them superstitious?
c. Cultural norms develop because a specific behavior is reinforced. Can you identify some behaviors that are typically reinforced in the United States that are not reinforced in other cultures? (For example, Korean business persons rarely smile at customers because people who smile in public are thought to look like fools.)

Try It!

Think about which schedule works best for completing items on an assembly line, assuming workers are paid for each item assembled.
a. Which schedule works best in a casino when someone plays the slot machines?
b. Which schedule works best when someone has to baby sit a child for a certain number of hours?

Try It!

One very good way to illustrate the existence of cognitive maps is to draw a map of the campus, or the layout in general of the community in which you live. Compare your map with that of other students, and then compare them to a formal map.

Try It!

Apply reinforcement principles to the "real world" problem--waste recycling. How would you engineer better paper recycling on a university campus? In a college dorm? In a selected neighborhood?

(E. S. Geller, J. L Chaffee, and R. E. Ingram, "Promoting Paper Recycling on a University Campus," *Journal of Environmental* Systems, 1975, 5, 39-57.)

Chapter 7 - Memory

MEMORY
Memory is an
<u>active process</u>
for
receiving,
encoding,
storing,
organizing,
altering, and
retrieving information.

SENSORY, SHORT-TERM & LONG-TERM MEMORY
Human memory can be pictured as three separate storage systems.
Different strategies are required to make the best use of each system.

MEMORY AND THE BRAIN
Consolidation is the process by which memories are formed in the brain. Engrams (relatively permanent memory traces) appear to be formed during a critical period after learning. Until they are consolidated, long-term memories are easily destroyed.

MEMORY LIMITATIONS
Everyday memories are not always accurate. Limitations of memory that sometimes appear to be flaws are actually adaptive and desirable in most circumstances.
It is not necessarily beneficial for us to remember "everything".

EIDETIC IMAGERY
The ability to retain a "projected" mental image long enough to use it as a source of information is commonly known as "photographic memory".

IMPROVING MEMORY
Memory can be improved by using: feedback (knowledge of results), recitation (summarizing aloud), rehearsal (mentally reviewing). Selecting and organizing information, spacing practice, and overlearning material also contribute to improving memory.

FORGETTING
The inability to retrieve information originates in a variety of circumstances.

MEASURING MEMORY
Remembering is not an all-or-nothing process. Information that appears to be lost may still reside in memory. Memory is not always complete. Partial memory is demonstrated in a variety of ways.
<u>Recall</u>: An ability to supply or reproduce information with a minimum of external cues.
<u>Recognition</u>: An ability to correctly identify previously learned information.
<u>Relearning</u>: The ability to learn again something that was previously learned.

ENCODING FAILURE
Often, memory failures occur because information wasn't stored in the first place. It wasn't attended to at sensory or short-term memory and was not encoded and stored.

CUE DEPENDANCY
Many of our memories rely on cues in the environment including the bodily state that we are experiencing as we attempt to encode and store memories (state-dependent learning).

SENSORY MEMORY (SM)

Sensory organs collect and transmit information to short term memory where it is retained for a short period of time.
Information is held as an exact copy of what is seen (an icon – ½ second) or heard (an echo – 2 seconds).
Generally, information is held just long enough to be moved to the next storage system.
Selective attention (focusing on a portion of sensory input) controls what information moves to the next level.

RECODING

STM is limited as to how much meaningful information can be retained. The average is 7 bits of information.
Recoding increases STM by organizing information into chunks (grouped bits of information such as in telephone numbers).

SHORT-TERM MEMORY (STM)

STM is a temporary storehouse for small amounts of information for brief periods. It is working memory, where we do much of our thinking.
If the information is not attended to, or is not sufficiently important, it is "forgotten".

REHEARSAL

Short-term memories disappear very rapidly. Silently repeating or mentally reviewing information to hold it in short-term memory is known as maintenance rehearsal. Without rehearsal, short-term memories disappear after 18 seconds. The more a short-term memory is rehearsed, the greater the likelihood that it will be stored in LTM.
Elaborative rehearsal links new information with existing memories and knowledge.

LONG-TERM MEMORY (LTM)

LTM is the large storehouse of relatively permanent storage of information that was important to us in some way at one time.

LONG TERM MEMORY TYPES

It is becoming clear that more than one type of long-term memory exists.
Procedural memories: conditioned responses and learned skills.
Declarative memories: contain specific factual information.
Semantic memories: a subpart of declarative memory that records impersonal knowledge about the world.
Episodic memory: a subpart of declarative memory that records personal experiences.

RECOVERED MEMORIES

Some memories of abuse that return to awareness appear to be genuine. However, caution is warranted when "recovered" memories are the only basis for believing that a person was sexually abused during childhood.

INTERFERENCE

Interference refers to the tendency for:
Retroactive interference: New learning impairs retrieval of older memories.
Proactive interference: Old learning interferes with new memory.

DECAY

Memory traces (changes in nerve cells or brain activity) fade over time and lack of use.

PSYCHOLOGICAL MOTIVES

Repression or suppression of information may occur for psychological reasons.

Chapter 7:
Memory

Practice Exam

1. Transforming incoming information into a usable form is the stage of memory called
   a. retrieval.
   b. encoding.
   c. storage.
   d. organization.

2. In order for a memory to be useful, it must be
   a. filed.
   b. episodic.
   c. decoded as an image.
   d. retrieved.

3. The kind of memory that lasts for only a second or two is
   a. long-term memory.
   b. short-term memory.
   c. eidetic memory.
   d. sensory memory.

4. The memory system used to hold small amounts of information for relatively brief time periods is called _____ memory.
   a. sensory
   b. short-term
   c. long-term
   d. tactile

5. Information in long-term memory is generally stored on the basis of
   a. images.
   b. meaning.
   c. sound.
   d. space.

6. Keeping a short-term memory alive by silently repeating it is called
   a. constructive processing.
   b. rehearsal.
   c. chunking.
   d. iconing.

7. Organizing information into larger units as a way of improving the efficiency of short-term memory is called
   a. chunking.
   b. categorization.
   c. verbal labeling.
   d. symbolization.

8. Which of the following would be considered a semantic memory?
   a. your first car
   b. the sixteenth president
   c. your third job
   d. the accident you saw three weeks ago

9. The average number of "bits" of information that short-term memory can usually handle is
   a. one.
   b. four.
   c. seven.
   d. ten.

10. Which of the following would be considered an episodic memory?
    a. 4 x 7 = 28
    b. the sixteenth president
    c. the accident you saw three weeks ago
    d. number of CDs owned

11. Often, memories appear to be available but not accessible, as in
    a. the tip-of-the-tongue phenomenon.
    b. sensory memory failure.
    c. engram decay.
    d. interference.

12. The storage capacity of long-term memory is best described as
    a. a single item.
    b. about seven items.
    c. about seven volumes.
    d. limitless.

13. Which of the following methods of measuring memory is being used when a student is required to recite poetry verbatim?
    a. recognition
    b. relearning
    c. recall
    d. serial position

14. Remembering the first and last items of a list better than items in the middle is due to
    a. the tip-of-the-tongue phenomenon.
    b. redintegration.
    c. the serial position effect.
    d. the pseudo-memory effect.

15. When new learning disrupts the ability to recall past, stored information, _____ has been said to occur.
    a. proactive interference
    b. disinhibition
    c. retrograde amnesia
    d. retroactive interference

16. As shown by the curve of forgetting, memory loss occurs
    a. as learning is still going on.
    b. very rapidly at first and then levels off to a slow decline.
    c. not until three to four hours after the learning trial is over.
    d. slowly at first but is essentially complete within one hour.

17. False memories of _____ have recently been profoundly evident resulting in numerous lawsuits.
    a. alien abduction
    b. radioaction exposure
    c. childhood sexual abuse
    d. being abandoned as a child

18. The worst that happens when hypnosis is used as an aid to memory in solving a crime is that
    a. the subject is not susceptible to hypnotic suggestion.
    b. the hypnotized subject's memory is no better than in a waking state.
    c. testimony based on hypnotic induction is not believed by juries.
    d. additional memories are produced that are largely false.

19. The inability to recall events preceding an accident involving injuries to the head is called
    a. retrograde amnesia.
    b. prograde amnesia.
    c. motivated forgetting.
    d. cognitive blockage.

20. A device that acts as a system or aid to improving memory is called a
    a. mnemonic.
    b. retriever.
    c. cue.
    d. memorizer.

Try It!
Report a "flashbulb" memory that is especially vivid for you. What role did emotion play in the formation of the memory? Have you rehearsed and retold the memory unusually often? How can flashbulb memories be explained?

Try It!
Psychology Today has surveyed its readers regarding their earliest memories. Ninety-six percent of the respondents reported having memories prior to the age of six, with sixty-eight percent reporting recall for events occurring when they were two or three. Further, a surprising seven percent said they had memories prior to age one, and a few even claimed to have prenatal recollections as well as memories of their own birth! While some of the early memories were of traumatic experiences (such as the birth of a sibling, being injured, or the death of relatives or pets), the majority of recollections were of more mundane things (like being given a bath, having a picture taken, or being pushed in a swing). Interestingly, most of the memories involved images rather than events. People remembered things like curtains blowing in the breeze, a light shining on someone's face, and a mobile hanging in the air. This is probably because small children generally lack the language skills necessary to encode a complicated series of events. Many psychologists, in fact, believe that it is rare for people to remember things that occurred before they were able to talk.

Now, write the answer to the same question *Psychology Today* asked its readers: "What is your earliest memory and how old were you?" Before starting, you need to be cautioned to try to make sure that it is a real memory and not something you've been told about or seen in photograph albums, etc. After you've finished, you should share your responses with some of your classmates. For more details see E. Stark, "Thanks for the Memories," *Psychology Today*, November, 1984.

Try It!
Meaning and Memory
The following exercise shows how varying degrees of meaning result in corresponding amounts of recall. Follow the directions given below, gather the data, answer the discussion questions on page 58, and then meet in class for a review of the concepts involved.

A. Background and Purpose

   Psychologists have found that meaningful information is easier to remember than that which is not. This is because it is associated with information that is already in memory. The purpose of this project is to show that material which is higher in association value is easier to store in memory and recall.

B. You will be testing subjects with three word lists. One list has high association value, the second has medium value, and the third has low association value. Each subject will be given all three lists; however, they should be given one at a time, at separate times, with some time interval between the administration of each list. The subjects will be asked to write down as many words as they can remember after hearing the list once.

C. Directions

1. Select three subjects for this study. They should be over ten years of age.

2. You need to meet with each subject three times to administer each of the three word lists.

3. Provide the subject with a pencil and sheet of paper.

4. Give each subject the high association word list first, then the medium list, and finally the low. Each should be given separately with a time interval in between.

5. Read the word list to the subject. Read the words in order, slowly, about one word per second. Practice this by yourself ahead of time to get the timing right.

6. The subject should listen carefully. After you complete reading the list, have the subject write down as many as he/she can remember. Do the same for each list.

7. Record the results for each subject on each word list. Find the average number of words recalled correctly for each type of list.

8. Answer the questions about your results, discussing what you found, and relating it to the material on memory in the text.

Word Lists

High	Medium	Low
the	bee	yad
dog	nor	cif
ate	can	mul
two	but	bix
and	fee	pog
did	lob	zel
not	sit	riv
eat	old	mib
for	doe	daf
you	run	hib

Results

Subject	Scores (number of correct words)		
	High	Medium	Low
1.			
2.			
3.			
Average Score			

D. Discussion

1. Based on the data you gathered, to what extent does association play a part in memory? Give reasons for your answer based on what you have learned about remembering and forgetting.

2. What are the implications of an associationistic theory of memory for student learning?

3. Give some examples of how a student might organize his/her study to take advantage of the association value inherent in the material.

Chapter 8 - Cognition, Language, and Creativity

COGNITION, INTELLIGENCE, and CREATIVITY

How we think, communicate, and solve problems are essential elements of being human.

COGNITION

The process of thinking or mentally processing information is known as cognition.
Cognition is influenced by how the information is mentally represented.
Representation may be done in the form of images (often a mental representation that has a picture-like quality),
concepts (ideas that represent a group of objects or events that allow us to think abstractly), and
symbols. Words or symbols and the rules for combining them are language.
Language is an especially powerful way to encode information and manipulate ideas.

LANGUAGE

Most cognition relies heavily on language. Words encode (translate) the world into symbols that are easy to manipulate. Language is primarily a human characteristic.

ANIMAL COMMUNICATION & LANGUAGE

Animals generally communicate through cries, gestures, and calls. Animals are capable of rudimentary language use, but only with the aid of human intervention.

CONCEPT FORMATION

A concept is an idea that represents a class of objects or events. By classifying information into meaningful categories, we form concepts.
A variety of concept types and conceptual rules dictate how we learn concepts.

POSITIVE & NEGATIVE CONCEPTS

Some concepts are based on experience with positive and negative instances (examples that either belong, or do not belong to a category).
Children often learn from positive and negative cases.

RELATIONSHIPS

Relational concepts are based on how an object relates to something else or how its features relate to one another (larger, left, north, inside-out, etc.).
Disjunctive concepts are defined by the presence of at least one of several possible features (must be blue, must have four wheels, etc.)

INTELLIGENCE

An overall capacity to think rationally, act purposefully, and deal effectively with the environment is a common definition of intelligence.

INTELLIGENCE TESTING

Linguistic, logical, mathematical, and spatial abilities are measured in traditional IQ testing. Intelligence tests provide a useful but narrow estimate of real-world intelligence.

MEANING

Denotative meaning is the exact dictionary definition of a word or concept; its objective meaning.
Connotative meaning is the subjective, personal, or emotional meaning of a word or concept.

ARTIFICIAL INTELLIGENCE

Any artificial system (often a computer program) that is capable of human-like problem solving or intelligent responding is referred to as artificial intelligence (AI).

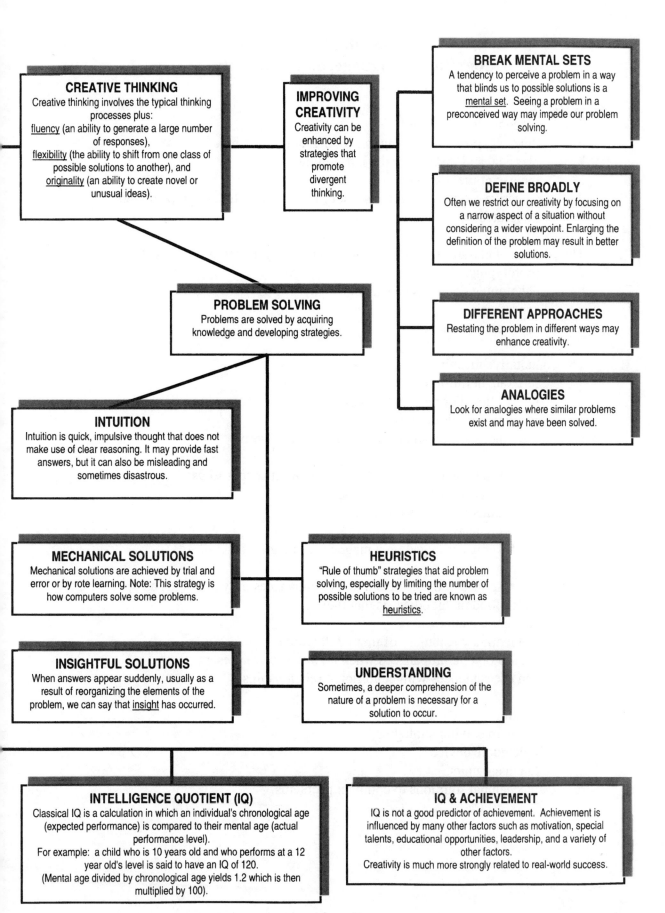

CREATIVE THINKING
Creative thinking involves the typical thinking processes plus:
fluency (an ability to generate a large number of responses),
flexibility (the ability to shift from one class of possible solutions to another), and
originality (an ability to create novel or unusual ideas).

IMPROVING CREATIVITY
Creativity can be enhanced by strategies that promote divergent thinking.

BREAK MENTAL SETS
A tendency to perceive a problem in a way that blinds us to possible solutions is a mental set. Seeing a problem in a preconceived way may impede our problem solving.

DEFINE BROADLY
Often we restrict our creativity by focusing on a narrow aspect of a situation without considering a wider viewpoint. Enlarging the definition of the problem may result in better solutions.

DIFFERENT APPROACHES
Restating the problem in different ways may enhance creativity.

ANALOGIES
Look for analogies where similar problems exist and may have been solved.

PROBLEM SOLVING
Problems are solved by acquiring knowledge and developing strategies.

INTUITION
Intuition is quick, impulsive thought that does not make use of clear reasoning. It may provide fast answers, but it can also be misleading and sometimes disastrous.

MECHANICAL SOLUTIONS
Mechanical solutions are achieved by trial and error or by rote learning. Note: This strategy is how computers solve some problems.

HEURISTICS
"Rule of thumb" strategies that aid problem solving, especially by limiting the number of possible solutions to be tried are known as heuristics.

INSIGHTFUL SOLUTIONS
When answers appear suddenly, usually as a result of reorganizing the elements of the problem, we can say that insight has occurred.

UNDERSTANDING
Sometimes, a deeper comprehension of the nature of a problem is necessary for a solution to occur.

INTELLIGENCE QUOTIENT (IQ)
Classical IQ is a calculation in which an individual's chronological age (expected performance) is compared to their mental age (actual performance level).
For example: a child who is 10 years old and who performs at a 12 year old's level is said to have an IQ of 120.
(Mental age divided by chronological age yields 1.2 which is then multiplied by 100).

IQ & ACHIEVEMENT
IQ is not a good predictor of achievement. Achievement is influenced by many other factors such as motivation, special talents, educational opportunities, leadership, and a variety of other factors.
Creativity is much more strongly related to real-world success.

Chapter 8:
Cognition, Language, and Creativity

Practice Exam

1.   The term "cognition" includes
      a.   thinking, problem solving, reasoning, and dreaming.
      b.   classical and instrumental conditioning.
      c.   the use of memory systems.
      d.   an active process by which sensory input is selected, organized, and
            integrated.

2.   The process of classifying information into meaningful categories is called
      a.   prototyping.
      b.   developing denotative meaning.
      c.   synesthesia.
      d.   concept formation.

3.   The connotative meaning of a word is
      a.   its exact definition.
      b.   its emotional or personal meaning.
      c.   its dictionary definition.
      d.   the exact spelling and pronunciation of the word.

4.   The first truly successful method of teaching chimpanzees to use language used
      a.   conditional signals and symbols.
      b.   a computer with keys that stand for words.
      c.   sign language.
      d.   plastic chips arranged on a magnetized board.

5.   One recent response to the criticism that chimpanzees only use signs as operant
      responses for food or "goodies" is that they
      a.   can learn syntax.
      b.   can learn a vocabulary of up to 240 words.
      c.   sign to other chimpanzees when no humans are present.
      d.   can use sentences with conditional relationships.

6.   Heuristics are
      a.   problem solving strategies.
      b.   mnemonic devices.
      c.   language units.
      d.   mechanical solutions to complex problems.

7. Fixation is a
   a. mechanical way of solving a problem.
   b. way of using insight to solve a problem.
   c. mnemonic device.
   d. barrier to problem solving.

8. Artificial intelligence refers to
   a. memory chips implanted in the brain.
   b. computer programs performing things that require intelligence when done by people.
   c. phony intellectual abilities.
   d. extraterrestrial knowledge.

9. If a person receives approximately the same score when taking the same test on different occasions, the test is considered
   a. valid.
   b. reliable.
   c. operational.
   d. standardized.

10. If Jane's intelligence quotient is 100, we know that she has a
    a. perfect score on a set of age-related tests.
    b. test performance superior to 90% of other children the same age who took the test.
    c. mental age typical of children who have the same chronological age.
    d. mental age below those of children with the same chronological age.

11. The distribution of IQ scores
    a. is approximately normal or bell-shaped.
    b. shows that most people score between 80 and 100.
    c. reveals a difference in the average for men and women.
    d. falls off abruptly above 100.

12. The relationship (correlation) between IQ scores and school grades is
    a. about .50.
    b. very low.
    c. about .25.
    d. too variable to be of much importance.

13. Using IQ scores as the sole measure of giftedness
    a. is the quickest way to identify creative individuals.
    b. ignores special talents.
    c. ignores the poor adjustment that characterizes such persons.
    d. identifies only persons from upper socioeconomic levels.

14. The fact that fraternal twins are more similar in intelligence than ordinary siblings suggests the importance of
    a. common hereditary factors.
    b. common environmental factors.
    c. genetic effects.
    d. effects of intrauterine environment.

15. Which of the following would be recommended by an educational consultant to increase a child's IQ?
    a. Change the diet of the child.
    b. Provide enriched educational opportunities for the child.
    c. Coach the child on test-taking.
    d. Provide the child with increased physical exercise.

16. A school curriculum built on Howard Gardner's theory of intelligence would provide
    a. neuromuscular training because such skills underlie general intelligence.
    b. training in logic, rhetoric, philosophy, and math to strengthen the general factor in intelligence.
    c. emphasis on creative, artistic abilities rather than the traditional emphasis on cognitive abilities.
    d. a diverse curriculum with education in skills not traditionally associated with IQ.

17. An alternate term for creativity is
    a. heuristic problem solving.
    b. inductive thought.
    c. divergent thought.
    d. deductive thought.

18. The advice to "sleep on it" would relate to which stage of creative thinking?
    a. verification
    b. illumination
    c. incubation
    d. preparation

19. The correlation between IQ and creativity is
    a. very high.
    b. very low.
    c. zero.
    d. more positively correlated the higher the IQ.

20.   If you wanted to enhance creativity, you would want to
       a.   isolate yourself.
       b.   make a rash decision.
       c.   dig deeper into a problem with logic.
       d.   look for analogies.

Try It!

Richards and Siegler found that movement was the attribute most frequently cited by children as a criterion for life. Younger children rely heavily on qualities of life that are true of animals but not of plants. Older children cite attributes that are true of both plants and animals.

You can do a simple replication of part of the study by asking children of various ages: (4-11) "Can you tell me how things that are alive are different from things that are not alive?" List the attributes cited at each age and the percentage of children who mentioned them. This provides a nice picture of children's increasingly complex knowledge structures. Focus on how the development of knowledge and cognition can be best explained. (Richards, D. D. & Siegler, R.S. [1986]. "Children's understanding of the attributes of life." Journal of Experimental Child Psychology , 42, 1-22.)

Try It!

Charles Croll has interviewed children of different ages, asking them, "Is Santa Claus real? Why? Why not?" Ask children the same question regarding Santa, the Tooth Fairy, the Easter Bunny, magic, cartoon characters, animals, germs, and so forth. The percentage of children who respond correctly shows a nice progression through ages 4-7. This is an easy way for you to get a glimpse into the cognitive world of younger children.

Try It!

There are many ways in which fixation in problem solving can be illustrated. A typical problem is this: How could you put your left hand completely in your right hand pants pocket and your right hand completely in your left hand pants pocket at the same time while you are wearing the pants? (See bottom of this page for answer.)

A large number of problems similar to the preceding are offered by Eugene Raudsepp in a *Psychology Today* article. This article will provide you with an excellent collection of creativity problems to solve. The article appears in the July 1980 issue of *Psychology Today*: 71-75, 88-90.

Try It!

Mednick's Remote Associates Test (RAT) is a good example of a creativity test that combines divergent and convergent thinking. The RAT consists of groupings of three words. The words in each group have a single word in common associated with them. The object is to find that word. For example, if the words were, "shake, cow, and carton," the common element is "milk" (milkshake, milk cow, and milk carton). The items below are similar to the RAT. Think about the question of what distinguishes creative thought from other types of problem solving. The class may also want to discuss Does the RAT actually tests creativity?

The answer is to put the pants on backward, whereupon the task becomes quite easy. We often miss this solution due to conventions about the "right" way to wear a pair of pants.

1) ball home naval
2) stream goose town
3) dance ladder door
4) dog pepper rod
5) sand mouse door

6) ball shake lotion
7) puff whipped ice
8) bowling cushion hair
9) sun bulb sky
10) wrench stove line

Answers for the preceding items are: 1) base 2) down 3) step 4) hot 5) trap 6) hand 7) cream 8) pin 9) light 10) pipe.

Chapter 9 - Motivation and Emotion

MOTIVATION

The concept of <u>motivation</u> refers to internal processes that initiate, sustain, and direct activities. Motives and goals greatly influence what we do and how we use our energies. Learned habits, external cues and cultural values influence motivated behavior.

PRIMARY MOTIVES

Basic motives, such as hunger and thirst, are controlled by internal signals monitored within the brain. Primary motives are based on biological requirements for survival.

NEEDS & DRIVES

Many motivated activities begin with an internal deficiency known as a <u>need</u>.
Needs may cause an energized motivational state known as a <u>drive</u> to develop.

HOMEOSTASIS

A steady state of bodily equilibrium regarding such things as body temperature, chemical concentrations in the blood, and blood pressure, is referred to as <u>homeostasis</u>.

FOOD AND EATING

Hunger is a basic physiological need which involves a complex interplay between fullness of the stomach, blood sugar levels, metabolism in the liver, and fat stores in the body. The most direct control of eating comes from the hypothalmus.

MASLOW'S HIERARCHY

Maslow's hierarchy categorizes needs as either <u>basic</u> or <u>growth</u> oriented. Lower needs are assumed to dominate over higher needs.

DIET

A diet is not just something you go on to lose weight.
The types and amounts of food you regularly eat, and the content of the foods defines your current diet.
The most effective "diet" is one that changes eating habits and activity levels.

EMOTION

An emotion is a state characterized by three major elements:
physiological arousal,
outward behaviors (gestures, facial expressions, gestures, etc.), and subjective feelings.
Emotions can be disruptive, but overall they help us adapt to environmental challenges.

OVEREATING & UNDEREATING

Overeating and undereating may be a result of physiological factors. However, they are often related to emotional or cultural factors.

PHYSIOLOGY OF EMOTION

Physical changes associated with emotion are caused by adrenaline, and by activity in the autonomic nervous system (ANS). The Polygraph ("lie detector") measures emotional arousal by monitoring physiological changes in the body. The accuracy of the lie detector can be very low.

EXPLANATIONS FOR EMOTIONS

Emotions have been explained in a variety of ways by different researchers. Contemporary views of emotion emphasize the effects of cognitive appraisal. All of the elements of emotion are seen as interrelated and interacting.

PRIMARY EMOTIONS

Robert Plutchik's research indicates eight primary emotions: fear, surprise, sadness, disgust, anger, anticipation, joy, and acceptance. Each may vary in intensity.

STIMULUS MOTIVES

Stimulus motives appear to be innate, but are not strictly necessary for survival. They express our needs for stimulation and information. They include curiosity, exploration, manipulation, and physical contact.

SECONDARY MOTIVES

Many needs, drives and goals are learned. Learned motives help explain many activities such as music making, creating works of art or working to become an expert in our field.

PAIN & SEX

Primary motives typically come and go in fairly regular cyclical patterns. However, the drive to avoid pain is different since it is episodic as opposed to cyclic. Pain avoidance and pain tolerance are partially learned.

Many psychologists do not think of sex as a primary motive because sex is not necessary for individual survival (as are food, water, and air). The sex drive is unusual because it is non-homeostatic.

AROUSAL THEORY

Stimulus drives reflect needs for sensory input. Arousal theory states that an ideal level of bodily arousal will be maintained if possible. Optimal performance usually occurs at moderate levels of arousal. High arousal is best for simple tasks, while lower arousal is best for complex tasks.

SOCIAL MOTIVES

Success, money, possessions, status, love, approval, grades, dominance, power, or belonging are social motives. Social motives are learned through socialization and cultural conditioning. Such motives account for much of the diversity of human motivation.

SEXUAL RESPONSE PATTERNS

Sexual arousal is related to the body's erogenous zones. But mental and emotional reactions are the ultimate source of sexual responsiveness. Generally, male and female sexual responses are similar. Overall, women and men have equal potential for sexual arousal and women are no less physically responsive than men are. The peak of male sexual activity is around 18 years of age; the peak of female sexual activity is at a later age.

EATING DISORDERS

Anorexia nervosa (active self-starvation) and bulimia nervosa (binge-purge eating) tend to involve conflicts about self-image, self-control, and anxiety. Both disorders are serious and can cause physical damage or death.

OBESITY

Obesity is the result of internal and external influences, diet, emotions, genetics, and exercise. People with weight problems are just as likely to eat when they are anxious, angry, or sad, as when they are hungry.

BODY LANGUAGE

Basic emotional expressions appear to be unlearned. Facial expressions, body gestures, and movements all express feeling, by communicating emotional tone. Facial expressions are recognized around the world. Body positioning can reveal feelings that would normally be concealed.

A HAPPY AND FULFILLING LIFE

Subjective well-being (happiness) is related to general life satisfaction and to having more positive emotions than negative ones. Having an extraverted, optimistic, and worry-free personality and making progress toward goals are associated with happiness.

Chapter 9:
Motivation and Emotion

Practive Exam

1. In the motivational sequence, needs generate drives, which in turn activate
    a. goals.
    b. expectations.
    c. incentives.
    d. responses.

2. The balanced state of our bodies which is maintained by biological drives is called
    a. homosapiens.
    b. homeostasis.
    c. homogeneity.
    d. homophobia.

3. If a food causes sickness or simply precedes sickness caused by something else, a learned _____ may result.
    a. psychosomatic illness
    b. taste aversion
    c. anorexia
    d. specific hunger

4. The body structure most closely associated with thirst is the
    a. pancreas.
    b. pituitary gland.
    c. hypothalamus.
    d. limbic system.

5. Which of the following statements concerning the set point is TRUE?
    a. The set point is not as important to hunger as the "start" and "stop" systems in the brain.
    b. Your set point is the weight you maintain when you are lightly exercising in order to lose weight.
    c. Fat cells release leptin which, when carried in the bloodstream to the brain, acts as a signal to eat less.
    d. Set points are determined by early eating patterns.

6. Which of the following statements is TRUE of eating disorders?
    a. Eating disorders occur in women slightly more than they occur in men.
    b. Typically, people with eating disorders have a body image that is very close to people with normal eating habits.
    c. Eating disorders rarely disappear on their own and thus require professional help.
    d. Depression is the root cause of most eating disorders.

7. You and a friend play three hours of racquetball. Afterwards, you are most likely to prefer
    a. plain water.
    b. a slightly salty liquid.
    c. a beverage containing some alcohol.
    d. milk.

8. The period during which female animals are sexually receptive is called
    a. mensis.
    b. estrus.
    c. hormonal readiness.
    d. estrogen.

9. That humans need patterned and varied stimulation to maintain normal functioning is suggested by experiments in
    a. sensory deprivation.
    b. pattern preference.
    c. self stimulation.
    d. free choice.

10. For relatively simple tasks, _____ levels of arousal can improve performance.
    a. low
    b. moderate
    c. high
    d. excessive

11. Taking the spontaneous interest and satisfaction out of learning can be avoided by
    a. using small extrinsic rewards at first.
    b. waiting for necessary skills to develop on their own.
    c. increasing extrinsic incentives.
    d. the use of intrinsic rewards.

12. For maximum efficiency, changes in bodily rhythms should be accomplished
    a. as quickly as possible.
    b. by sleeping in several short sessions, as opposed to a single eight hour session.
    c. gradually over a period of days.
    d. by keeping a log of mood and energy levels.

13. What is the correct order of needs in Maslow's hierarchy?
    a. physiological; esteem; safety; self-actualization; love and belonging
    b. self-actualization; physiological; safety; love and belonging; esteem
    c. physiological; safety; love and belonging; esteem; self-actualization
    d. self-actualization; safety; love and belonging; esteem; physiological

14. Emotional expressions are
    a. a means of communicating one's feelings to others.
    b. culturally conditioned.
    c. not subject to the forces of evolution.
    d. all of these

15. "Shifty" eye movements are an indication of
    a. liking and disliking.
    b. general emotional tone.
    c. telling the truth or lying.
    d. none of these

16. Schachter's cognitive theory emphasizes the influence of _____ on emotion.
    a. labeling and interpretation
    b. parasympathetic arousal
    c. learned helplessness
    d. personality factors

17. A common bond between all of the theories of emotion described in the text is that they consider _____ an element of emotion.
    a. attribution
    b. kinesics
    c. cognition
    d. physiological arousal

18. The general emotional feelings telegraphed by the body include
    a. pleasantness-unpleasantness.
    b. attention-rejection.
    c. liking-disliking.
    d. activation (arousal).

19. Which theory claims that emotions are organized in the brain and that emotional feelings and bodily expressions occur simultaneously?
    a. the common sense theory
    b. the Cannon-Bard theory
    c. attribution theory
    d. the James-Lange theory

20. Which of the following concepts do modern theorists of emotion add to the classical models?
    a. physiological arousal
    b. labeling
    c. thinking
    d. appraisal

Try It!

An exercise can be developed around the results of a projective approach to assessing nAch. Find a somewhat ambiguous photo in a magazine and ask a subject (an adult) to write a short story telling what led up to the situation portrayed, what is happening now (including the feelings of the characters), and what will happen next. Keep track of the number of references to achievement themes and imagery (references to striving, trying, goals, excellence, success, planning, achievement, and so forth).

Try It!

Motivation—Need for Achievement (nAch)

The exercise on the next page deals with the need for achievement. This is near and dear to the hearts of students since you spend a great deal of time and energy in pursuit of goals that will satisfy this need. Take the following test to see where you are on the nAch scale.

This is a five-point rating scale. Your responses should be based on how you feel about each item at the present time. This is not an evaluation of your work in this course, and your responses will be anonymous. Try to respond as accurately as you can. Rate each item as follows:

not characteristic of me	1
seldom characteristic of me	2
sometimes characteristic of me	3
usually characteristic of me	4
very characteristic of me	5

1. I tend to be competitive and strive to excel in most activities I undertake. _____

2. I often go out of my way to take on outside responsibilities in the college and community. _____

3 When thinking about the future, I emphasize long-term goals more than short-term goals. _____

4. I get bored easily by routine. _____

5. I tend to get upset if I cannot immediately learn whether I have done well or poorly in any situation. _____

6. I am generally not a gambler; I prefer calculated risks. _____

7. In choosing a career, I would be more interested in the challenge of the job than in the pay. _____

8. When I cannot reach a goal I have set for myself, I strive even harder to reach it. _____

9. If given the choice, I would prefer a highly successful stranger as a co-worker to a friend as a co-worker. _____

10. I believe people should take personal responsibility for their actions. _____

TOTAL FOR THIS SCALE _____

nAch(oo!)

Pardon the pun! But just as the sneeze is a precursor of a cold, so some behaviors indicate the existence of a need and the intensity of the drive to satisfy it.

The items in this exercise describe some behaviors which are related to achievement motivation. People do not experience them all to the same degree, but put together they can be an indicator of the strength of the need for achievement. The highest possible score is 50 points; the lowest is 10. On the scale, achievement motivation could be evaluated as follows:

High: 40 - 50   Medium: 20 - 40   Low: 10 – 20

Try It!

If you, like most college students, hold down a job, list all of the major reasons that you have for working. (If you don't have a job, try this experiment on one of your friends who does go to school and have a job.) Then compare your motivations with what Sylvia Porter, in *New Money Book for the Eighties* (Avon Books, 1980), cites as being the 12 most-often mentioned reasons people give for working. In order of importance, these reasons are: 1) security, 2) interesting work, 3) opportunity for advancement, 4) recognition, 5) a good working environment, 6) wages, 7) autonomy, 8) making social contacts, 9) opportunity to learn new things, 10) good working hours, 11) ease of the job, and 12) fringe benefits. Your students probably placed wages a good deal higher than sixth. Do you feel that your motives for working will change after you finish school, and if so, how and why?

Try It!
Polygraph Tests
Respond to the following questions:
   a. How would you react if your employer were to demand regular polygraph tests of all employees?
   b. Should the polygraph be used to check up on government officials?
   c. What do you think about "lie detecting" in the future? How will it be different?

Chapter 10 - Personality

PERSONALITY
Each of us displays consistent behavior patterns that define how we are likely to behave. These unique and relatively stable behavior patterns are known as personality. Personality also refers to the special blend of talents, attitudes, values, hopes, loves, hates, and habits that make each of us a unique person.

UNDERSTANDING PERSONALITY
Identifying traits, probing mental conflicts and dynamics, noting the effects of prior learning and social situations, and knowing how people perceive themselves can help us understand personality.

PERSONALITY THEORIES
Psychodynamic theories: are based on the works of Sigmund Freud.
Behavioristic theories: seek to determine what makes learning experiences have a lasting effect.
Trait theories: many personality tests are based on trait theories.
Humanistic theories: focus on human problems, potentials, ideals, and the ability to change.

PSYCHODYNAMIC THEORIES
Pychodynamic theorists are not content with studying traits. Instead, they try to probe under the surface of personality to learn what drives, conflicts, and energies make us behave as we do.

LEARNING THEORIES
(Behavioral Approaches)
Behavioral personality theories emphasize that personality is a result of learning, conditioning, and the effects the environment.
Social learning theory adds cognitive elements in which expectancies and reinforcement value play a role.
Identification and imitation play a key role in learning to be "male" or "female".

FREUD & PERSONALITY
Sigmund Freud is the best known of the psychodynamic theorists.
To Freud, the personality is made up of the id, ego, and, superego.
Libido (derived from life instincts) is the primary energy running the personality.
The personality operates on three levels: unconscious, preconscious, and conscious.
Personality development is a result of a series of psychosexual stages, and fixation at any stage can have a lasting impact on personality.
Conflicts within the personality may cause anxiety and prompt the use of ego-defense mechanisms.

HUMANISTIC THEORIES
The humanistic approach emphasizes subjective experience, problems, potentials, and ideals.
Self-actualization (the process of fully developing personal potentials) plays an essential role in humanistic theory.
Humanism is optimistic and emphasizes free choice. It serves as a counterpoint to the static quality of trait theory, the pessimism of psychoanalytic theory, and the mechanical approach of behaviorism.

PERSONALITY TESTING

To measure and assess personality, psychologists use interviews, direct observation, questionnaires, and projective tests.

RELIABILITY, VALIDITY & OBJECTIVITY

Reliability is the ability of a test to yield nearly the same score each time it is given to the same person.
Validity is the ability of a test to measure what it says it is measuring.
A test is said to be objective when the same score is attained when different people score it.

SHYNESS

A tendency to avoid others combined with uneasiness and strain when socializing is known as shyness. Shyness involves public self-consciousness often related to a lack of social skills (a proficiency at interacting with others).
Changing unrealistic or self-defeating beliefs, and improving social skills can reduce shyness.

INTERVIEWS

Interviews may be structured or unstructured. They provide a great deal of information, but interviewer bias and misperceptions, along with the halo effect, may lower the accuracy of an interview.

PERSONALITY TRAITS

Stable qualities that a person shows in most situations are known as traits. Traits are inferred from behaviors and are often used to predict future behaviors (shy, sensitive, orderly, etc.).

DIRECT OBSERVATION

Placing an individual in a simulated real-life situation and observing their reactions can be very helpful in determining an individual's fitness for certain jobs (such as police "shoot-don't shoot " firearms training). Use of rating scales and objective recording of specific behaviors can overcome bias and misperception.

CLASSIFYING TRAITS

Traits are often described as being:
common (those shared by most members of a culture)
individual (which define a person's unique personal qualities)
cardinal (a trait so basic that all of a person's activities can be traced to that trait).
Note: Very few of us possess cardinal traits.

QUESTIONNAIRES

Personality questionnaires are typically paper-and-pencil tests that reveal personality characteristics. Single item responses are of little value. The patterns of responses are revealing. Questionnaires are objective and reliable, but their validity has been questioned. The results of more than one test are often used in clinical settings.

PERSONALITY TYPES

A personality type refers to people who have several traits in common (strong silent, athletic).

PROJECTIVE TESTS

During projective tests, a person is asked to respond to ambiguous stimuli or unstructured situations (the Rorschach inkblot test may be the most famous projective test). There are no "right" or "wrong" answers in these tests. Scoring the test relies on the scorer's interpretation of the responses.
Of the various personality tests, projective tests are considered to be the least valid. Objectivity and reliability are also low.

SELF CONCEPT

All of a person's ideas, perceptions, and feelings about their own personality traits is their self-concept.
A stable self-concept tends to guide what we pay attention to, remember, and think about.

Chapter 10:
Personality

Practice Exam

1. Psychologists regard personality as unique and
   a. changing.
   b. enduring.
   c. rigid.
   d. flexible.

2. Hereditary aspects of one's emotional nature are termed
   a. character.
   b. temperament.
   c. personality.
   d. somatotypes.

3. Which pairing is correct?
   a. psychodynamic - internal conflicts
   b. behavioristic - personal growth and subjective experience
   c. behavioristic - inner workings of personality
   d. humanistic - conditioning and learning

4. _____ theories stress private, subjective experience and personal growth.
   a. Trait
   b. Humanistic
   c. Behavioristic
   d. Psychodynamic

5. Which personality theories attempt to explain behavior by focusing on the inner workings of the personality including internal conflicts?
   a. trait
   b. behavioristic
   c. psychodynamic
   d. humanistic

6. Introverts and extroverts are
   a. personality traits.
   b. extremely rare.
   c. kinds of personality theorists.
   d. personality types.

7. Biological instincts and urges are represented in psychoanalytic theory by the
   a. id.
   b. superego.
   c. psyche.
   d. ego.

8. Which of the following is governed by the reality principle?
   a. id
   b. ego
   c. superego
   d. superid

9. The overly neat and orderly person is described by Freud as being
   a. orally retentive.
   b. anally retentive.
   c. a phallic personality.
   d. anally expulsive.

10. Characteristics that are shared by most members of a culture are termed
    a. cardinal traits.
    b. ethnic traits.
    c. general traits.
    d. common traits.

11. Attempts to answer the question, "What are the basic dimensions of personality?" have resulted in
    a. neo-Freudian theory.
    b. cognitive-behavioral models.
    c. the five-factor model.
    d. the trait-situation controversy.

12. If you know the personality of an identical twin, you can expect the personality of the other twin to be
    a. unrelated.
    b. similar.
    c. identical.
    d. conflicting.

13. To understand personality, trait theorists attempt to
    a. create traits that fit people.
    b. increase the number of basic traits that have been identified.
    c. classify traits and discover which are most basic.
    d. reduce the common traits to measures of temperament.

14. The 16PF designed by Cattell can be used to produce a _____ profile.
    a. personality
    b. surface
    c. central
    d. trait

15. _____ identified common, individual, cardinal, central, and secondary traits.
    a. Jung
    b. Eysenck
    c. Bem
    d. Allport

16. According to twin studies, the role of environment in shaping personality is
    a. small but detectable.
    b. just as or more important than heredity.
    c. overestimated.
    d. negligible.

17. A social learning approach to developing moral values in childhood would emphasize
    a. organismic valuing.
    b. conditions of worth.
    c. identification and imitation.
    d. the Oedipus and Electra conflicts.

18. Which point of view portrays human nature in positive terms and holds that self-actualization is possible?
    a. psychoanalytic
    b. behavioristic
    c. humanistic
    d. Jungian

19. Which of the following is a projective test?
    a. the MMPI-2
    b. Cattell's 16 PF
    c. any clerical aptitude test
    d. the Rorschach

20. Which of the following techniques is recommended for overcoming shyness?
    a. Accept that it is a basic personality trait that cannot be changed.
    b. Avoid asking open-ended questions of acquaintances.
    c. At first, one should avoid situations that lead to social contact.
    d. Practice social skills and be willing to take some social risks.

Try It!
Personality Traits

Attached is a list of terms that describe personality traits that are commonly found in the population. You can probably think of many others, but stick with these for this exercise.

The purpose of this exercise is to compare your own ratings of yourself with the ratings of others. Do others see you in the same way that you see yourself? Follow the directions to find out.

1. Make several copies of the list of terms. Ask three people to each separately rate you on the list of traits. You should also rate yourself. Select a variety of people to do the rating, such as a family member, a friend, a co-worker, a neighbor, a teacher, a spouse, etc.

2. You and each of your raters should select and check off 20 traits that describe you best. It may be hard to stick to 20, but force yourself (and your raters) to do so.

3. On the summary rating sheet, check off your choices and the choices of each of the raters.

4. Now you can compare how you see yourself with the way others see you. You can also compare the responses of the different raters. They may not all agree with you or with each other!

Personality Traits: Rating Sheet

Rater's I.D._____(Rater may wish to be anonymous.)

Identification of personality traits of _____

Instructions: Check the twenty (20) traits from this list that best describe the person named above. Your evaluation should be based on behavior that you have observed.

__boastful	__generous	__optimistic	__shy
__candid	__good-natured	__orderly	__sincere
__clumsy	__gracious	__outgoing	__skeptical
__compulsive	__grouchy	__patient	__sloppy
__considerate	__headstrong	__perceptive	__sly
__cooperative	__honest	__persistent	__smart
__cordial	__idealistic	__persuasive	__sociable
__courageous	__imaginative	__pessimistic	__studious
__courteous	__kind	__prejudiced	__suspicious
__crafty	__logical	__prideful	__tactful
__daring	__loyal	__punctual	__tense
__dependable	__mature	__reasonable	__truthful
__diligent	__methodical	__rebellious	__understanding
__efficient	__modest	__reliable	__unselfish
__energetic	__naive	__respectful	__vain
__ethical	__neat	__sarcastic	__versatile
__forgetful	__nervous	__sexy	__warm
__friendly	__open-minded	__short-tempered	__wholesome

Personality Traits: Summary Sheet

In order to compare your own rating of yourself with the ratings of others, put your own twenty (20) checks on this chart first. Then put each rater's checks in the boxes provided.

	RATERS			
	ME	1	2	3
boastful				
candid				
clumsy				
compulsive				
considerate				
cooperative				
cordial				
courageous				
courteous				
crafty				
daring				
dependable				
diligent				
efficient				
energetic				
ethical				
forgetful				
friendly				
generous				

	RATERS			
	ME	1	2	3
good-natured				
gracious				
grouchy				
headstrong				
honest				
idealistic				
imaginative				
kind				
logical				
loyal				
mature				
methodical				
modest				
naive				
neat				
nervous				
open-minded				
optimistic				
orderly				

Personality Traits: Summary Sheet (cont.)

	RATERS			
	ME	1	2	3
outgoing				
patient				
perceptive				
persistent				
persuasive				
pessimistic				
prejudiced				
prideful				
punctual				
reasonable				
rebellious				
reliable				
respectful				
sarcastic				
sexy				
short-tempered				
shy				
outgoing				
patient				

	RATERS			
	ME	1	2	3
sincere				
skeptical				
sloppy				
sly				
smart				
sociable				
studious				
suspicious				
tactful				
tense				
truthful				
understanding				
unselfish				
vain				
versatile				
warm				
wholesome				
sincere				
skeptical				

Personality Traits: Evaluation

Now you need to evaluate the results. The following questions should help you.

1. Overall, does <u>your</u> selection of traits present a favorable or unfavorable picture of your personality?

2. Do the traits identified by <u>your raters</u> present a favorable or unfavorable picture?

3. How different are the traits selected by your raters from yours? In what ways do they differ?

4. How do you explain the difference?

5. Which of your traits appear to be most <u>positive</u> based on all ratings?

6. Which of your traits appear to be most <u>negative</u> based on all ratings?

7. What do you think about this type of evaluation of personality? Explain what you mean.

Try It!

Personality Types

The following is an Introversion-Extroversion scale developed by the Michael Sosulski..

INTROVERTED? EXTROVERTED? WHICH ARE YOU?

To find out, mark true (T) or false (F) next to each of the statements below, and then follow the scoring instructions.

____1) I tend to keep in the background at social events.

____2) I prefer to work with others rather than alone.

____3) I get embarrassed easily.

____4) I generally tell others how I feel regardless of how they may take it.

____5) I really try to avoid situations in which I must speak to a group.

____6) I am strongly motivated by the approval or interest of others.

____7) I often daydream.

____8) I find it easy to start conversations with strangers.

____9) I find it difficult to make friends of the opposite sex.

____10) I particularly enjoy meeting people who know their way around the social scene.

____11) I would rather read a good book or watch television than go out to a movie.

____12) I would rather work as a salesperson than as a librarian.

____13) I spend a lot of time philosophizing and thinking about my ideas.

____14) I prefer action to thought and reflection.

____15) I am often uncomfortable in conversations with strangers.

____16) I am mainly interested in activities and ideas that are practical.

____17) I would prefer visiting an art gallery over attending a sporting event.

____18) I enjoy open competition in sports, games, and school.

____19) I make my decisions by reason more than by impulse or emotion.

____20) I have to admit that I enjoy talking about myself to others.

____21) I like to lose myself in my work.

____22) I sometimes get into arguments with people I do not know well.

____23) I am very selective about who my friends are.

____24) I make decisions quickly and stick to them.

Scoring:

1. Go through the odd-numbered items and add the number of true and false responses. Put the numbers in the appropriate boxes.

2. Go through the even-numbered items, adding the true and false responses. Enter the numbers in the proper boxes.

3. Add only the ODD-false items to the EVEN-true items.

4. The total thus obtained should be marked on the introversion-extroversion scale.

ODD ITEMS	True	False			
		True	False	EVEN ITEMS	
	TOTAL				

INTROVERT				EXTROVERT	
0	6	12		18	24

Try It!

You can simulate a Rorschach test by making your own ink blots. Take a large bottle of a dark-colored liquid and an eyedropper. Fold a sheet of paper in half, then open it up. Put a few drops of the liquid into the fold and close it, pressing it flat. More than one application of drops may be needed to create a blot that is symmetrical and large.
Show your blots to several persons not in your class and record their responses. Ask your subjects to respond to both the overall image and to particular parts of it.

Chapter 11 - Health, Stress, and Coping

HEALTH, STRESS, AND COPING

A variety of personal habits and behavior patterns affect health. Stress (the mental and physical condition that occurs when a person must adjust or adapt to the environment) is a part of everyday life. How we cope with stress will affect the quality of our lives.

HEALTH PSYCHOLOGY

Health psychology is the study of how behavioral principles can be used to prevent illness and promote health.
Psychological principles are also applied to management of existent medical problems.

STRESS, STRESSORS, AND PRESSURE

Stress is the mental and physical condition that occurs when a person must adjust or adapt to the environment.
A stressor is the condition or event in the environment that challenges or threatens a person.
Pressure occurs when a person must meet urgent external demands or expectations (when there is a deadline or a short period to make a response to a stressor).

BEHAVIORAL RISK FACTORS

Maintaining good health is a personal responsibility, not a matter of luck.
Some lifestyles promote health and others lead to illness or death.
Behaviors that increase the chances of disease, injury or early death are behavioral risk factors.
Wellness is based on minimizing these factors and engaging in health-promoting behaviors.

APPRAISING STRESSORS

When we decide if a stressor is relevant or irrelevant (or a threat or challenge) we are making a primary appraisal.
When we assess our resources and choose a way to cope with a threat or challenge, we are performing a secondary appraisal.
A perception that we have no control over the threat or challenge increases the stress reaction.

REFUSAL SKILLS

Training in refusing to smoke, drink, or take drugs can be important in reducing these behavioral risk factors.

LIFE SKILLS

Life skills training teaches stress reduction, self-protection, decision making, self-control, and social skills.

EMOTION-FOCUSED

When we attempt to control our emotional reactions to situations, we are using emotion- focused coping.

SAFE SEX

Relatively small changes in behavior can almost completely eliminate the health hazard of unsafe sex.
Use of condoms, refraining from sex with drug users or other high-risk partners, and reducing the number of partners are all behaviors that reduce the risk of sexually transmitted diseases, including AIDS.

PROBLEM-FOCUSED

When our coping is aimed at managing or altering the distressing situation itself, we are employing problem-focused coping.

BAD STRESS / GOOD STRESS

Much of what we call "stress" may come about as a result of unpleasant events.
However, stress is not necessarily "bad". Forms of stress related to positive activities such as recreational activities, dating, or moving to a sought-after job are referred to as eustress.

MANAGING STRESS

The damaging effects of stress can be reduced with stress management techniques.
Exercise, meditation, progressive relaxation, modifying ineffective behaviors, and avoiding upsetting thoughts allow us to manage stress more effectively.

STRESS & HEALTH

Long-range susceptibility to accident or illness appears to be related to multiple life changes.
Immediate psychological and mental health is more closely related to the intensity and severity of daily hassles (microstressors).
Intense or prolonged stress may cause damage in the form of psychosomatic disorders (illnesses in which psychological factors contribute to bodily damage).

LEARNED HELPLESSNESS & DEPRESSION

Learned helplessness is a learned inability to overcome obstacles or to avoid punishment, or learned passivity and inaction to aversive stimuli. People who are made to feel helpless in one situation are more likely to act helpless in other situations. Learned helplessness has been used as a model for understanding depression. Mastery training acts as an antidote to helplessness.

DEFENSE MECHANISMS

A defense mechanism (commonly referred to as "ego defense mechanism") is a habitual and often unconsious psychological process used to help us avoid, deny, or distort sources of threat or anxiety, including threats to a person's self-image.

CONFLICT

Conflict occurs when a person must choose between contradictory needs, desires, motives, or demands.
Approach-approach conflicts occur when we must choose between two desirable alternatives.
Avoidance-avoidance conflicts happen when we must choose between two undesirable alternatives.
Approach–Avoidance conflicts occur when a single goal has elements that both attract and repel us.
Double approach-avoidance conflicts in which each alternative has both positive and negative qualities are very common in everyday living.

SOURCES OF STRESS

Frustration and conflict are often the origins of stress.

FRUSTRATION

Frustration occurs when a person is prevented from reaching a goal.
External frustration may be from sources outside the individual that impede progress (traffic jams, finding that the item you wanted is out of stock).
Personal frustrations are based on personal characteristics over which a person perceives they have no control.

REACTIONS TO FRUSTRATION

Aggression is one of the most persistent and frequent responses to frustration. Aggression may be direct or displaced onto a target other than the actual source of frustration. Scapegoating refers to blaming a person or group of people for conditions that they had nothing to do with. Other reactions to frustration include persistence, circumvention and escape or withdrawal.

Chapter 11:
Health, Stress, and Coping

Practice Exam

1. A graduate student in psychology who decides on a career applying psychological knowledge to medical problems is choosing
    a. behavioral medicine.
    b. psychoneurology.
    c. health psychology.
    d. neurophysiology.

2. Health psychology is the
    a. study of the ways in which psychological principles can be used to prevent illness and promote health.
    b. use of psychological principles and research methods to solve practical problems.
    c. study of how individuals behave, think, and feel in the presence, actual or implied, of others.
    d. study of behavioral factors in medicine, physical illness, and medical treatment.

3. Emotional exhaustion, depersonalization, and reduced personal accomplishment describe people who are experiencing
    a. grief following death or disaster.
    b. unemployment.
    c. job burnout.
    d. sensory deprivation.

4. Ultimately, stress depends upon
    a. how a situation is perceived.
    b. whether or not the somatic nervous system is involved.
    c. how the limbic system interprets the situation.
    d. having a Type A personality.

5. Primary appraisal refers to the stage in emotional adjustment during which
    a. the means of meeting a threat is chosen.
    b. the pros and cons of a particular course of action are weighed.
    c. one decides if a situation is threatening or not.
    d. vague feelings of anxiety begin.

6. Stress is likely to occur whenever
    a. anger or rage occurs.
    b. persistent or stereotyped responding is required of an organism.
    c. an organism is forced to distinguish between real and imagined barriers.
    d. demands are placed on an organism to adjust or adapt.

7. Which of the following qualifies as an escape or withdrawal response from frustration?
   a. drug use
   b. persistence
   c. displacement
   d. redintegration

8. Scapegoating refers to
   a. the use of apathy as a means of dealing with conflict.
   b. habitual redirection of aggression to some person or group.
   c. a tendency to blindly repeat an unsuccessful response.
   d. the act of attributing personal frustration to external causes.

9. Which of the following conflicts is most like those we encounter in everyday life?
   a. double frustration-avoidance
   b. partial avoidance
   c. double ambivalent-avoidance
   d. double approach-avoidance

10. A basic defense mechanism in which one refuses to accept an unpleasant reality is
    a. intellectualization.
    b. rationalization.
    c. denial.
    d. reaction formation.

11. When "the new baby" arrives home, an older brother begins to use baby talk and to wet the bed. His behavior demonstrates
    a. compensation.
    b. repression.
    c. reaction formation.
    d. regression.

12. The most costly event on the Social Readjustment Rating Scale is
    a. divorce.
    b. death of spouse or child.
    c. retirement.
    d. jail term.

13. Hypochondriacs suffer from
    a. overactive endocrine glands.
    b. feelings of inferiority.
    c. imaginary diseases.
    d. stress-induced diseases.

14. With which problem has biofeedback been most effective as a treatment?
    a. headache
    b. excessive sleep syndrome
    c. heart disease
    d. hyperactivity

15. Increased risk for heart attack is associated with
    a. depersonalization.
    b. job burnout.
    c. Type A personality.
    d. physically-demanding work.

16. The final stage of the general adaptation syndrome is
    a. exhaustion.
    b. engagement.
    c. disengagement.
    d. alarm.

17. One of the most effective techniques for relaxing is
    a. exercise.
    b. progressive relaxation.
    c. guided imagery.
    d. meditation.

18. A person who is unusually resistant to the effects of stress would be described by psychologists as
    a. hardy.
    b. detached.
    c. vulnerable.
    d. Type A.

19. Symptoms like fatigue, loss of appetite, and lack of energy are characteristic of the _____ in the G.A.S.
    a. alarm reaction
    b. stage of resistance
    c. stage of exhaustion
    d. stage of avoidance

20. Upsetting thoughts and emotions may have a negative influence on health through their link with the
    a. sensory and psychomotor systems.
    b. thalamic stress projection system.
    c. brain and immune system.
    d. stage of alarm and resistance.

Try It!

In recent years, there has been an epidemic of kids killing kids. In what ways might frustration have led to many of these acts of violence? How might children be taught to manage their frustration in ways other than lashing out violently (and often fatally) at their peers? What other causes can you identify?

Try It!

To study the topic of conflict, it might again be valuable to create a little conflict among your friends. Ask if one of them would like to play a "game of chance" with you. Tell him/her that you are going to flip a coin. If it comes up heads, you will take him/her out to lunch three times. If it is tails, he/she has to take you out to lunch five times. Give your friend a few moments to decide if he or she still wants to play. Think about the approach-avoidance conflict that has been created.

Chapter 12 - Psychological Disorders

PSYCHOLOGICAL DISORDERS
Psychological disorders damage the quality of life, in varying degrees, for many people.
Psychological disorders are complex and have multiple causes.

INSANITY
Insanity is a legal term referring to a mental inability to manage one's own affairs or to be aware of the consequences of one's actions.

WHAT IS NORMAL?
Determining abnormality can be tricky. Several factors may be taken into consideration before a diagnosis is given:
subjective discomfort (personal, private feelings of discomfort, unhappiness, or emotional distress),
statistical abnormality (abnormality defined on the basis of an extreme score on some dimension, such as IQ, anxiety, compulsive behavior, etc.),
social non-conformity (whether the behavior is consistent with the social norms),
situational context (under some circumstances a behavior may be acceptable, while in other situations it is not- starting a forest fire may be arson, or it might be a fire-fighting technique), and
maladaptiveness (behaviors that make it difficult to adapt to the environment and meet the demands of day-to-day life).

CLASSIFYING MENTAL DISORDERS
The most widely used classification system is the Diagnostic and Statistical Manual of Mental Disorders (DSM-IV-TR, 2000).
The manual standardizes terminology for mental health workers, organizes mental disorders into categories, provides statistical information, and assists diagnosis.

PERSONALITY DISORDERS
Personality disorders are deeply ingrained patterns of behavior are that are maladaptive (impair the individual's ability to function adaptively or productively).
These patterns typically begin as early as childhood.
Personality disorders cited in the DSM-IV include: the dependent, narcissistic, borderline, and paranoid personalities.

ANXIETY-BASED DISORDERS
Anxiety refers to feelings of apprehension, dread, or uneasiness. Anxiety is appropriate in some circumstances. Anxiety that is out of proportion to a situation may reflect a psychological problem.
Anxiety-based disorders include adjustment, generalized anxiety, obsessive-compulsive, stress, dissociative and somatoform disorders.

ANTISOCIAL PERSONALITY
One personality disorder that is often mentioned and frequently misunderstood is the anti-social personality.
Individuals with this disorder lack a conscience. The are impulsive, selfish, dishonest, emotionally shallow and are manipulative
These individuals are frequently referred to as sociopath or psychopath.
The childhood of a sociopath frequently reflects emotional deprivation, neglect and physical abuse.
They are rarely treated successfully.

ANXIETY-BASED DISORDERS EXPLAINED
Anxiety-based disorders appear to be partially inherited. Explanations for some anxiety-based disorders come from four major psychological perspectives.
Psychodynamic: emphasizes unconscious conflicts as the cause of disabling anxiety.
Humanistic: emphasizes the effects of a faulty self-image.
Behaviorism: emphasizes the effects of previous learning (particularly avoidance learning).
Cognitive: focus on distorted thinking, judgement, and attention.

SUICIDE

Taking one's own life is a relatively frequent cause of death that can, in many cases, be prevented.
Suicide is the seventh highest cause of death in North America. For every 2 people who die in a homicide, 3 take their own lives.

PREVENTION

Suicide can often be prevented by the efforts of family, friends, and mental health professionals. Knowing the common characteristics of suicidal thoughts and feelings will give you some guidance in talking to a suicidal person.

CAUSES

The major psychological approaches offer explanations for mood disorders. Research continues, but heredity is clearly an element contributing to susceptibility to mood disorders.

MOOD DISORDERS

Mood disorders involve disturbances of mood or emotion. Manic or depressive states are produced separately, or in some combination.

DELUSIONAL DISORDERS

A psychosis where severe delusions are present is a delusional disorder. Not normally present are the hallucinations, extreme emotional reactions or personality disintegration found in other psychotic disorders (even though a break with reality is very clear).
The main feature of delusional disorders is the presence of firmly held false beliefs (many of which involve some degree of paranoia).

PSYCHOTIC DISORDERS

Psychotic disorders, the most severe forms of psychopathology, involve emotional extremes or breaks with reality.
Typical psychotic episodes can include hallucinations, delusions, disturbed communication and personality disintegration, mania, depression, and schizophrenia.
An organic psychosis is based on known injuries or diseases of the brain (often caused by poisoning, drug abuse, and dementia).

SCHIZOPHRENIA

Schizophrenia is a psychosis characterized by delusions, hallucinations, apathy, and a wide difference between thought and emotion.
Personality disintegration is often a significant element of schizophrenia.
NOTE: Motion pictures and television often incorrectly use the terms schizophrenia and "multiple personality". They are NOT the same psychiatric problem.

SCHIZOPHRENIC TYPES

Schizophrenia appears to be a group of related disturbances with four major subtypes:
Disorganized type is marked by extreme personality disintegration, and bizarre behavior. The ability to function socially is impaired.
Catatonic type is associated with withdrawal from social activity. Mutism, odd postures and sometimes-violent behaviors occur.
Paranoid type (the most common type) demonstrates outlandish delusions of persecution or grandeur.
Undifferentiated type shows prominent psychotic symptoms, but none of the specific features of catatonic, disorganized, or paranoid types.

CAUSES

Schizophrenia appears to originate from multiple sources. Explanations include combinations of childhood trauma, environmental stress, an inherited susceptibility, and abnormalities in the brain.

95

Chapter 12:
Psychological Disorders

Practice Exam

1. An inability to behave in ways that foster the well-being of the individual and ultimately of society defines
    a. insanity.
    b. psychopathology.
    c. self-destructiveness.
    d. social nonconformity.

2. Jared is an artist who lives a unique lifestyle and is considered to be eccentric, creative, and unusual. Distinguish this type of non-traditional person from others who have not adopted the usual minimum rules for behavior, which is destructive. This example illustrates one of the problems with what definition of normality?
    a. social nonconformity
    b. statistical
    c. cultural
    d. subjective discomfort

3. An important use of DSM-IV is as a(n)
    a. aid in the selection of therapy.
    b. guide to research on possible causes of mental disorders.
    c. statistical encyclopedia of the incidence of various forms of violent crime.
    d. accurate guide to who should be determined insane for legal reasons.

4. Sexual and gender identity disorders include difficulties in all BUT which of the following areas?
    a. paraphilias
    b. sexual identity
    c. homosexuality
    d. sexual dysfunction

5. Which of the following personality disorders describes a person who may use excessive emotional and attention seeking behavior?
    a. dependent
    b. histrionic
    c. narcissistic
    d. schizoid

6. The antisocial personality
    a. avoids other people as much as possible.
    b. is relatively easy to treat effectively by psychotherapy.
    c. tends to be selfish and lacking in guilt.
    d. usually gives a bad first impression.

7. In the United States and Latin America, Latinos use the term _____ to refer to chronic psychosis.
   a. mania
   b. hispania
   c. locura
   d. agua

8. A disorder characterized by continuous tension and occasional anxiety attacks in which persons think they are going insane or are about to die is called a
   a. panic disorder.
   b. phobia.
   c. depressive psychosis.
   d. hysterical reaction.

9. A ritualistic act that a person feels compelled to perform is called a/an
   a. obsession.
   b. compulsion.
   c. phobia.
   d. regression.

10. A disorder that is a delayed reaction to a catastrophic event is called
    a. obsessive-compulsive disorder.
    b. post-traumatic stress disorder.
    c. adjustment psychosis.
    d. dissociative disorder.

11. The dissociative disorder known as *fugue* refers to
    a. physical flight to escape conflict.
    b. severe depression.
    c. hallucinations.
    d. obsessive behavior.

12. The primary characteristic of psychotic behavior is
    a. being dangerous to oneself or others.
    b. subjective discomfort.
    c. the degree of incapacitation.
    d. loss of contact with reality.

13. False beliefs that are held even when the facts contradict them are called
    a. hallucinations.
    b. psychopathic tendencies.
    c. delusions.
    d. regressions.

14. Multiple personality or dissociative identity disorder often begins
    a.   as a result of combat exhaustion.
    b.   in adulthood as a response to unremitting phobias.
    c.   as a consequence of post-traumatic stress disorders.
    d.   in childhood, as a result of unbearable experiences.

15. A young adult who shows little emotional expression, withdraws from social activities and displays delusions and inappropriate affect is most likely a
    a.   manic.
    b.   schizophrenic.
    c.   multiple personality.
    d.   paranoid.

16. Regarding hereditary influences and schizophrenia, it is most accurate to say that
    a.   heredity has been ruled out as a factor in schizophrenia.
    b.   some people may inherit a potential for schizophrenia.
    c.   the children of schizophrenic parents are least likely to become schizophrenic.
    d.   if one identical twin is schizophrenic, the other will be at some time in his or her life.

17. Suffering from a bipolar I disorder, a person is
    a.   hyperactive, agitated, incoherent.
    b.   in a state of total despair.
    c.   in a state of "waxy flexibility."
    d.   suffering from delusions of persecution.

18. The treatment for seasonal affective disorders is
    a.   thorazine.
    b.   electro-convulsive therapy.
    c.   injections of melatonin.
    d.   bright lights.

19. The likelihood that biological factors, especially brain chemicals, may be involved in mood disorders is suggested by
    a.   the effectiveness of lithium carbonate in the treatment of depression.
    b.   the bipolar nature of many mood disorders.
    c.   traditional Freudian psychoanalytic theories.
    d.   behavioral studies of learned helplessness.

20. Which of the following is a misconception about suicide?
    a.   More women than men commit suicide.
    b.   Suicidal people give no warning.
    c.   College students are most likely to attempt suicide during final exam periods.
    d.   all of these

Try It!

Think of examples of odd or unusual behavior you have observed in public. After thinking of several examples, return to each and ask yourself if there is any set of circumstances under which the behavior observed might be considered normal. (For example, the person observed had lost a bet, was undergoing an initiation, was practicing a part for a play, was part of a psychology experiment, etc.) The point is that the behavior may have been truly eccentric, and perhaps pathological, but that few behaviors are universally normal or abnormal.

Try It!

The text mentions that there is a case on record of four identical quadruplets all of whom developed schizophrenia. The odds against this happening are truly staggering. Identical quadruplets occur only once in every sixteen million births, and less than half of them survive to adulthood; only one in a hundred of these is schizophrenic, and the odds against all of them being schizophrenic seem overwhelming. This case, then, could seem to provide evidence for the heritability of schizophrenia. Keep in mind, however, that the quadruplets shared many other things besides their genes. For example, they all shared their mother's uterus where they could have contracted a viral infection or been exposed to some chemical substance. They all had the possibly brain-damaging liability of being born with very low weights. All of them were placed in incubators and spent the first six weeks of their lives in a hospital. They all grew up with constant publicity surrounding their daily activities. Finally, they all shared a father who was known for eccentric and erratic behavior and who remained extremely close to them even into adulthood. Look into this case more carefully. See a report on the twenty-year follow-up on this unusual and interesting case by M. S. Buchsbaum, "The Genain Quadruplets," *Psychology Today* August 1984.

Chapter 13 - Therapies

SEEKING HELP

Everyone should know how to obtain high-quality mental health care in his or her community. Most communities have a variety of services available.

The yellow pages will list psychologists, psychiatrists, and counselors.

Concerned citizens who keep listings of qualified therapists and services often organize mental health associations. Crises hotlines are staffed by volunteers trained to provide information about resources available.

THERAPIES

Psychotherapy facilitates positive changes in personality, behavior, and adjustment.

ORIGINS OF THERAPY

Evidence shows that stone-age man attempted some form of cure for apparent mental problems.

During the Middle Ages, treatments for mental illness focused on demonology. Before the development of modern therapies, superstition dominated attempts to treat psychological problems. Sigmund Freud developed the first modern psychotherapy early in the 20th century.

DIMENSIONS OF THERAPY

Psychotherapy can be done in various ways. Therapies may treat individuals or groups. They may be directive or non-directive. Some therapists assume an active role, while others focus on the client attaining their own insight into the origins and solutions to their problems. Some therapies are open-ended while others are time-limited with only a limited number of sessions being scheduled.

PSYCHOANALYSIS

The main goal of psychoanalysis is to resolve internal conflicts that lead to emotional suffering. Freud relied on four basic techniques to uncover the unconscious roots of neurosis. Traditional psychoanalysis called for three to five therapy sessions a week. Treatment often lasted years. Psychoanalysis has become rare due to the large expense and extensive time involved.

HUMANISTIC THERAPIES

Humanistic therapies tend to be optimistic. They assume that it is possible for people to use their potentials fully and live fulfilling lives.

GESTALT THERAPY

Gestalt therapy emphasizes immediate awareness of thoughts and feelings. Its goal is to rebuild thinking, feeling, and acting into connected wholes, and to help clients break through emotional blockages.

CLIENT-CENTERED THERAPY

Client-centered therapy is a non-directive form of therapy based on insights gained from conscious thoughts and feelings.

Carl Rogers, the founder of client-centered therapy, outlined four basic conditions for effective therapists to maintain.

Unconditional positive regard refers to an ability to give unqualified acceptance to another person.

Empathy is an ability to take another persons point view; to feel what another person is feeling.

Authenticity refers to the ability of therapists to be genuine and honest about their own feelings.

Reflection is the process of rephrasing or repeating thoughts and feelings expressed by clients so they can become aware of what they are saying.

EXISTENTIAL THERAPY

Existential therapy focuses on the problems being in the world (existing) where there are choices to make. Existential therapy focuses on free will, the human ability to make choices. Existential therapists believe you can choose to become the person you want to be.

COMMON FEATURES

Common features of all therapies include:
a caring relationship between the client and the therapist,
a protected setting in which the client is free to express fears or anxieties without fear of rejection,
an explanation or rational for the client's suffering along with a proposed line of action to end the suffering, and
a new perspective about themselves and their situation with a chance for the client to practice new behaviors.

BEHAVIOR THERAPY

Behavior therapy uses learning principles to make constructive changes in behavior, particularly maladaptive behavior.

BEHAVIORAL TREATMENTS

Behavior therapists assume that people have learned to be the way they are. If they have learned to behave in problematic ways, they can change by relearning more appropriate responses.

COGNITIVE THERAPY

Maladaptive thoughts, beliefs, and feelings often underlie emotional and behavioral problems. Cognitive therapists make a step-by-step effort to correct negative thoughts that lead to depression or similar problems.

AVERSION THERAPY

Aversion therapy involves suppressing an undesirable response by associating it with an aversive stimulus.

GROUP THERAPY

Most therapies can be adapted for group situations Group therapies can be as effective as individual therapy. Groups do offer some special benefits not found in individual therapies.

DESENSITIZATION

Systematic desensitization involves use of classical conditioning to overcome fears (such as phobias) and anxieties. In desensitization, gradual adaptation and reciprocal inhibition are used to break the link between fear and particular situations.

MEDICAL THERAPIES

Anything from a brief crisis to a full-scale psychosis can be treated with psychotherapy. The major depressive disorders, schizophrenia, or other severe conditions are more often treated medically by psychiatrists (a medical doctor with specialization in mental disorders).
Treatments using drugs, electroconvulsive therapy, or surgery intended to alter the brain (psychosurgery) are done under the supervision of psychiatrists.

OPERANT THERAPY

Learning principles of positive reinforcement, non-reinforcement, shaping, and removal of the rewards that maintain undesirable behaviors are used in operant therapies. Positive reinforcement in the form of tokens (symbolic rewards such as plastic chips or merit points) is often used to obtain the most effective results.

Chapter 13:
Therapies

Practice Exam

1. Psychotherapy is best viewed as
   a. the best way to undo the past in order to correct severe problems.
   b. a major overhaul of the psyche.
   c. a way to make constructive changes.
   d. applicable only to those with psychological problems.

2. The early technique used to release "evil spirits" from the skull of an emotionally disturbed individual, called trepanning, also may have been used to
   a. conduct witchcraft.
   b. conduct surgery.
   c. kill people who were unusual since many people did not survive the "treatment."
   d. none of these

3. The first true psychotherapy was developed by _____ around the turn of the century to treat cases of _____ .
   a. Freud; hysteria
   b. Pinel; psychosis
   c. Eysenck; neurosis
   d. Bicétre; hysteria

4. Which form of therapy places responsibility for the course of therapy on the client?
   a. insight therapy
   b. action therapy
   c. directive therapy
   d. non-directive therapy

5. The purpose of free association and dream analysis is to
   a. encourage relaxation.
   b. tap the unconscious.
   c. discover the patient's defense mechanisms.
   d. provide unlimited positive regard.

6. Total and uncritical acceptance of a client's thoughts and feelings is called
   a. empathic understanding.
   b. unconditional positive regard.
   c. reflection.
   d. transference.

7. The concepts of free will, choice, meaning, freedom, and isolation are most closely identified with
    a. existential therapy.
    b. non-directive therapy.
    c. psychoanalysis.
    d. transactional analysis.

8. One advantage of telephone therapy is that it
    a. deals with crises between sessions.
    b. advises clients briefly.
    c. offers brief support to clients.
    d. all of these

9. The principal assumption of behavior therapy is that
    a. all types of therapy are ultimately based on classical conditioning.
    b. unconscious conflicts can be uncovered and unlearned.
    c. problems in behavior are learned and can be changed.
    d. symptoms cannot be alleviated until the causes are determined.

10. Gradually approaching a feared stimulus while maintaining relaxation describes
    a. a time-out procedure.
    b. a token economy.
    c. systematic desensitization.
    d. rational-emotive therapy.

11. To maximize the effects of a token economy, the therapist tries to focus on specific
    a. fears and anxieties.
    b. unconditioned responses.
    c. target behaviors.
    d. response-contingent punishments.

12. The behavioral technique that has been most effective in treating depression is
    a. aversion therapy.
    b. a token economy.
    c. cognitive therapy.
    d. covert sensitization.

13. A cognitive therapist is concerned primarily with helping clients change their
    a. thinking patterns.
    b. behaviors.
    c. life-styles.
    d. habits.

14. Which is true of group therapy?
    a. A person can act out, as well as talk about, problems.
    b. Little, if any, support is provided by other group members.
    c. Group therapy is not like real-life situations.
    d. Group therapy requires supervision by several therapists at once.

15. To help clients understand the feelings of others, therapists using psychodrama may use
    a. role reversals.
    b. reflection.
    c. role playing.
    d. transference.

16. The goal of sensitivity groups is to
    a. reinforce appropriate behavior in other group members.
    b. have group members act out current life problems.
    c. take part in exercises designed to increase awareness of oneself and others.
    d. engage in brutally honest discussion to tear down defenses and false fronts.

17. A common criticism of pharmacotherapy in the treatment of psychoses is that
    a. drug therapies result in lengthened hospitalization.
    b. it is much more expensive than alternative forms of therapy.
    c. it is wrong to treat the symptoms and not the cause.
    d. it is easily overused.

18. The drugs used to control hallucinations and other psychotic symptoms are called
    a. anti-depressants.
    b. energizers.
    c. minor tranquilizers.
    d. antipsychotics.

19. Psychosurgery is rarely used for treatment of mental illness because
    a. regrowth of brain cells slowly reverses effects of the procedures.
    b. electroconvulsive therapy has replaced it.
    c. it is irreversible and unpredictable.
    d. it has been shown to have little or no effect on personality.

20. Compared to another type of psychotherapist, a psychiatrist is more likely to
    a. prescribe drugs.
    b. charge lower fees.
    c. do psychotherapy.
    d. rely on Rogerian, client-centered, techniques.

Try It!

For one week, keep a "daydream journal" by jotting in the margin of your notes the topic of any daydreams you have. At the end of a week, evaluate your daydreams. What are the themes? How frequently do the daydreams occur? What do the dreams say about your feelings toward this course or other events in your lives? Do they reveal unconscious desires, as postulated by Freud?

Try It!
Behavior Modification

Form a small group with your classmates or friends outside of class (three per group would be ideal), and work on a plan to change a behavior. Each of the three should have a behavior to change. The group can work on each one. There is an advantage to a group rather than an individual working on the problem, because it is more likely to get done if the group works on it. It also gives support to each individual in the planning and executing of the change.

In preparation for this project, you may need to review the basic concepts of operant conditioning. In particular, go over reinforcement so that you are clear on how it is to be applied. Got to the work sheet on the next page.

Behavior Self-Modification: Worksheet

In this exercise, you will identify a behavior you want to change, and the group will help you to develop a plan of action to bring this about. You should do the following:

1. Each person in your group should identify a behavior he/she would like to change. Keep it simple. Try something like nail biting, smoking, a poor study habit, or overeating. You can certainly think of others.

2. Use the outline that follows as a guide for developing your program for change. First you should describe the present situation; then you can work on changes. Keep in mind that you should try to do only what is possible. There is no point in planning what you won't carry out.

I. The Present Situation

   A. The problem behavior: Here you should briefly but clearly state what behavior you wish to change. It should be described exactly as it occurs, indicating frequency, circumstances, and how you feel when doing it.

   B. The stimulus cues: These are the stimuli in your environment that have become associated with the behavior you wish to change. An example: smoking while drinking a cup of coffee. If you want to stop smoking, you will have to change that whole behavior pattern, because coffee drinking and smoking have become associated. What are all the cues or stimuli that are associated with the undesirable behavior? You should try to identify as many of these as possible. It may be a good idea to do some self-observation, taking notes of the circumstances that surround the behavior you want to change. (If you are doing this assignment over a long period of time, keep a log for several days to be sure you don't miss the significant cues.)

   C. The reinforcements: You will need to identify the immediate and delayed reinforcements for the behavior you want to change. Be honest about this, and try to identify what they are. For example, smoking relaxes you and makes you feel good; it looks cool; it gives you something to do with your hands; you can blow neat smoke rings, etc.

II. Changes That You Plan to Make

   A. The new behavior that you want to develop to replace the old: Remember, you can't just stop doing something. You need to do something different in its place. An overeater doesn't stop eating, but eats differently! A smoker doesn't stop breathing, but inhales differently! Describe the new behavior. It needs to be attainable.

   B. New stimulus cues: Objects or events you plan to associate with the new behavior to help it become established.

C. <u>The reinforcements for the new behavior</u>: These need to be both immediate and long range. Plan specific reinforcements and set specific times when they will be received.

D. <u>Behavioral changes</u>: No behavioral changes occur in a vacuum. The new behavior and the new stimulus cues that are associated with it should constitute a total change in your lifestyle or approach to whatever you are changing. For example, to lose weight or maintain a desired weight you have to change not only how much you eat, but what, when, and where you eat. You also have to change your way of thinking about food. Your new behaviors, reinforcements, etc., have to reflect a total commitment to the new style for it to have a lasting effect.

Try It!

The following exercise will give you first-hand experience in locating mental health services in his or her own area. This could pay big dividends later. Everyone needs at some time to think about getting, or helping someone get, professional psychological help. In a crisis a person may not have the time or opportunity to do a thorough review of what is available in the area. Being prepared is a great advantage. Go to the next page to read the scenario and fill out the worksheet.

A Friend in Need: Assignment Sheet

You have a friend who has a serious adjustment problem. It has reached the point where he/she can no longer do his or her work, is having serious problems with his or her family, is generally miserable and very anxious. Thoughts of suicide recur, and he/she has started to drink heavily. He/she knows you are studying psychology and asks you for some assistance in finding professional help. The friend indicates that he/she has some money, but is on a limited budget.

Research the resources that would be available in the city and county to help the friend. You should identify specific sources of help and know something about the kind of assistance that would be provided. This means you should visit the facility, talk to personnel there, read brochures, etc., to become well informed.

Indicate the resources which you have found. Note where you found out about each and how you checked it out.

State briefly what services your friend could expect from each of the resources, who is eligible for the services, and what the fees might be. This will require a personal visit, a phone call, or at least reading some literature provided by the office or agency.

What do you think of the possibilities of your friend getting the kind of help he/she needs, based on what is available in your area? Explain your answer.

Chapter 14 - Social Behavior

SOCIAL BEHAVIOR
Social psychology studies how we behave, think, and feel in social situations.

SOCIAL INFLUENCE
A major fact of social life is that our behavior is influenced in numerous ways by the actions of other people. Our desire to remain part of a group may overcome our better judgement.

ATTITUDES
Attitudes are mixtures of belief and emotion that predisposes us to respond to other people, objects, or institutions in positive or negative ways.

AFFILIATION
A basic human trait is a desire to affiliate with other people.
The need to affiliate is based on human desires for approval, support, friendship, and information.

LIFE IN SOCIAL GROUPS
We are born into an organized society with established values, expectations, and behavior patterns. Each person in a society is a member of many overlapping social groups.

INTERPERSONAL ATTRACTION
Interpersonal attraction is the basis for most voluntary social relationships.
Proximity, frequent contact, beauty, competence, and similarity affect interpersonal attraction.

STRUCTURE, COHESION & NORMS
Structure (the network of roles, communication, and power in a group),
cohesiveness (the degree of attraction among group members and our desire to remain members of the group), and
norms (the accepted standard of conduct) influence our behaviors within groups.

GROUP ROLES
Social roles (patterns of behavior expected of persons in various social positions) may be ascribed (not under our control) or achieved (roles we have chosen for ourselves).

SELF-DISCLOSURE
Self-disclosure is essential for developing close relationships.

LOVING & LIKING
Romantic love is associated with high levels of interpersonal attraction, heightened arousal, mutual absorption, and sexual desire.
Liking someone involves a relationship based on intimacy, but lacking passion and commitment.

CONFORMITY
The groups, of which we are members, may prompt us to conform (to bring our behavior into agreement or harmony with the norms or behaviors of others in the group).
Sanctions (rewards and punishments) administered by groups enforce conformity among the members.

OBEDIENCE
A special type of conformity to the demands of an authority is known as obedience.

AGGRESSION

Aggression is a fact of life. Explanations of human aggression are varied.

Ethologists argue that humans have a "killer instinct" inherited from our animal ancestors.

Biological explanations emphasize brain mechanisms and physical factors as triggers for aggression.

The frustration-aggression hypothesis states that frustration tends to lead to aggression.

Social Learning theory suggests that some aggression may derive from behaviors that are modeled for us.

BYSTANDER APATHY

The unwillingness of bystanders to offer help during emergencies is known bystander apathy. Bystanders are reluctant to help when they perceive that others are likely to do so (diffusion of responsibility) or when they lack empathy for the victim.

FORMING ATTITUDES

Direct contact (personal experience), interaction with others (being influenced by discussions with others who hold particular beliefs), group membership (affiliation with others), mass media (magazines, television), and chance conditioning (conditioning that takes place by chance or coincidence) may all play a role in attitude formation.

ATTITUDE CHANGE

Although attitudes are relatively stable, they are learned, and can be changed.

COGNITIVE DISSONANCE

Cognitive dissonance occurs when there is clash between our self-image, thoughts, beliefs, attitudes or perceptions and our behavior. We change our attitude to resolve the feeling of discomfort we experience.

ATTITUDES THAT INJURE

Prejudice is a negative emotional attitude held toward members of a specific social group. Scapegoating (blaming another person or group for conditions that they had nothing to do with) is a common origin of prejudice.

REDUCING PREJUDICE

Prejudice is reduced by equal-status contact with other groups and by mutual interdependence, which promotes cooperation.

People may set aside petty differences when one superordinate goal (natural disasters, wars, etc.) exceeds or overrides all other goals.

Prejudices are difficult to maintain during and after attempts to meet superordinate goals.

PERSUASION

Persuasion is any deliberate attempt to change attitudes or beliefs through information and arguments.

To persuade others, you must be aware of your role as a communicator, the characteristics of the audience, and the type of message that will appeal to them.

COMPLIANCE

The term compliance refers to situations in which one person bends to the requests of someone who has little or no authority.

Assertiveness training may help us become more direct and honest in our expression of feelings and desires in order to overcome being compliant in ways that make us unhappy.

BRAINWASHING

Cults and other coercive groups sometimes use forced attitude change (brainwashing).

Brainwashing requires a captive audience that is isolated from other people who would support their original attitudes. The target must be completely dependent on the captors, and the indoctrinator must be in a position to reward the captive for changes in attitudes or behavior.

Cults often recruit individuals who are vulnerable (mildly depressed or perhaps alienated from friends and family).

111

Chapter 14:
Social Behavior

Practice Exam

1. According to the text, social psychology is the study of how people
   a. form organized social groups.
   b. behave in the presence of others.
   c. affect the behavior of others.
   d. relate to social institutions.

2. The degree of attraction among group members relates to the dimension of
   a. compatibility.
   b. structure.
   c. cohesiveness.
   d. conformity.

3. In attribution theory, the unstated expectations that define appropriate behavior in various settings are known as
   a. external causes.
   b. situational causes.
   c. social affirmations.
   d. situational demands.

4. Solomon Asch's classic experiment (in which subjects judged a "standard" line and "comparison" lines) showed that
   a. subjects conformed to the group about two-thirds of the test trials.
   b. subjects were not nervous or upset about making judgments different from the group.
   c. seventy-five percent yielded to group pressure at least once.
   d. when tested alone only ten percent made errors of judgment.

5. Studies of conformity indicate that people are more apt to be influenced by others if they
   a. are concerned about the approval of others.
   b. have low needs for certainty and structure.
   c. are in temporary rather than established groups.
   d. are in very large groups.

6. The real danger of "groupthink" is that it
   a. is contagious.
   b. occurs in cohesive groups.
   c. disrupts coordinated efforts at group problem solving.
   d. leads to a suspension of critical thinking.

7. Approximately what percentage of the subjects in Milgram's original "shocking" experiment went all the way to the 450 volt level?
   a. 95 percent
   b. 65 percent
   c. 45 percent
   d. 25 percent

8. Subjects in Milgram's experiment who gave large shocks rationalized that they were NOT personally responsible for their actions. This raises questions about our willingness to commit inhumane acts as a result of
   a. coercive power.
   b. obedience to a legitimate authority.
   c. expert power.
   d. conformity to group pressure.

9. The person who agrees to a small request initially is more likely later to comply with a larger demand. This describes the
   a. door-in-the-face-effect.
   b. foot-in-the-door effect.
   c. low-ball technique.
   d. high-ball technique.

10. A learned disposition to respond to people, objects, or institutions in a positive or negative way defines
    a. cognitive dissonance.
    b. socialization.
    c. attitudes.
    d. stereotypes.

11. Any deliberate attempt to bring about an attitude change by the transmission of information is called
    a. groupthink.
    b. coercion.
    c. persuasion.
    d. brainwashing.

12. A major reason for the ability of role playing to change attitudes is that it
    a. lacks realism and emotional impact.
    b. generates cognitive dissonance.
    c. creates a need for multiple selves.
    d. immediately and dramatically changes one's beliefs.

13. Cognitive dissonance is usually strongest when the reward is
    a. significantly delayed.
    b. ambiguous.
    c. large.
    d. small.

14. Prejudice based on displaced aggression represents a form of
    a. projection.
    b. discrimination.
    c. scapegoating.
    d. authoritarianism.

15. A classroom experiment using eye color to produce prejudice demonstrated that
    a. development of prejudice is slow but noticeable.
    b. reversing prejudice, like creating it, is a slow process.
    c. status inequalities encourage prejudice.
    d. young children are immune to prejudice.

16. Creation of superordinate goals has been shown to be effective in reducing
    a. intergroup conflict.
    b. authoritarianism.
    c. cognitive dissonance.
    d. social posturing.

17. Integrated classrooms most effectively reduce racial prejudice when children are made mutually
    a. interdependent.
    b. competitive.
    c. persuasive.
    d. superordinate.

18. Studies of prosocial behavior show that the more potential helpers present in an emergency, the
    a. more likely people are to get involved.
    b. lower the chances are that help will be given.
    c. greater the personal responsibility felt by those present.
    d. greater the risk of personal injury to potential helpers.

19. The empathy-helping relationship is a concept that refers to
    a. counseling.
    b. therapy.
    c. the more we "feel for" a person, the more likely we will help them.
    d. the less we identify with a specific group, the more likely we are to help.

20. A behavior such as altruism is explained by sociobiologists through the
    a. direct passing on of altruistic genes from generation to generation.
    b. increased chance that relatives of an altruistic person will survive.
    c. learning of such behaviors by children as they model themselves after adults.
    d. use of imprinting and critical period concepts.

Try It!

Violate a social norm. For example, you could ask to pay more than the asking price for a pint of milk or offer to help pay for a part of someone else's food while waiting in a cafeteria line. How do others react?

Try It!

Make two columns on a sheet of paper. In one column, list some "good" prejudices that you personally hold, and in the other, list "bad" prejudices that you have. Then discuss with the class what prejudice is and whether there can be "good" and "bad" prejudices.

Try It!

Aggression is a part of everyone's experience and is the subject of the following exercise. It is becoming a serious social problem in American society while the causes are not well understood. Television violence has been a subject of much discussion, and lots of statistics are quoted for its frequency.

Consider the question of violence on television. Form a definition of violence. Then determine what kinds of behavior you would characterize as violent. Both of these should be noted on the data sheet on the next page. Then, watch one hour of television each night of the week for one week, observing the number of violent acts in that show's episode. Record your findings on the worksheet below.

Aggression on Television: Data Sheet

Definition of violence: _____
_____
_____

Some examples of behavior that is evidence of violence on TV:
_____
_____
_____

Make a note of the programs you watched during the week and the number of violent acts you observed.

PROGRAM	DAY	TIME	NUMBER OF VIOLENT ACTS

Appendix - Behavioral Statistics

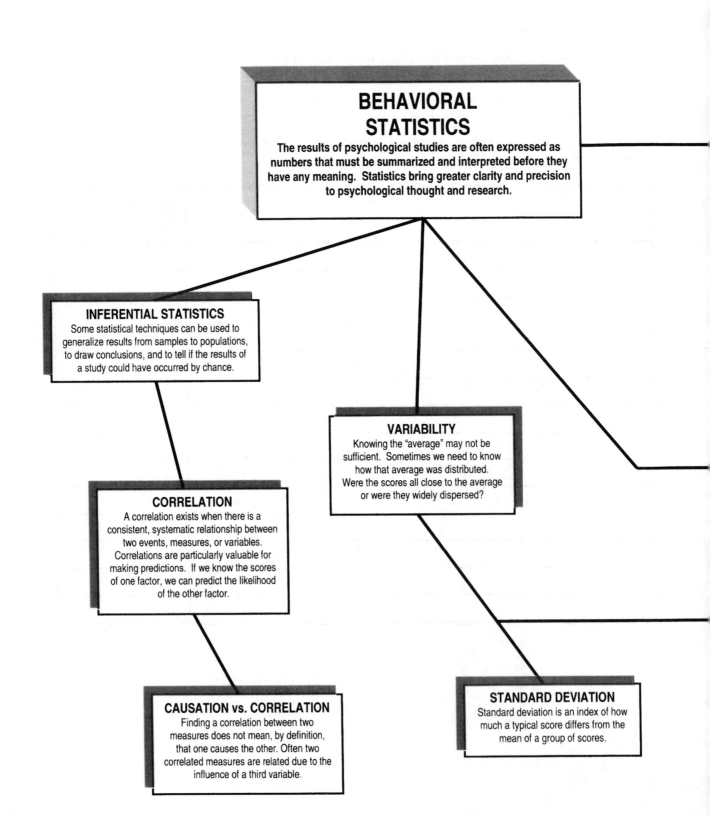

BEHAVIORAL STATISTICS
The results of psychological studies are often expressed as numbers that must be summarized and interpreted before they have any meaning. Statistics bring greater clarity and precision to psychological thought and research.

INFERENTIAL STATISTICS
Some statistical techniques can be used to generalize results from samples to populations, to draw conclusions, and to tell if the results of a study could have occurred by chance.

CORRELATION
A correlation exists when there is a consistent, systematic relationship between two events, measures, or variables. Correlations are particularly valuable for making predictions. If we know the scores of one factor, we can predict the likelihood of the other factor.

VARIABILITY
Knowing the "average" may not be sufficient. Sometimes we need to know how that average was distributed. Were the scores all close to the average or were they widely dispersed?

CAUSATION vs. CORRELATION
Finding a correlation between two measures does not mean, by definition, that one causes the other. Often two correlated measures are related due to the influence of a third variable.

STANDARD DEVIATION
Standard deviation is an index of how much a typical score differs from the mean of a group of scores.

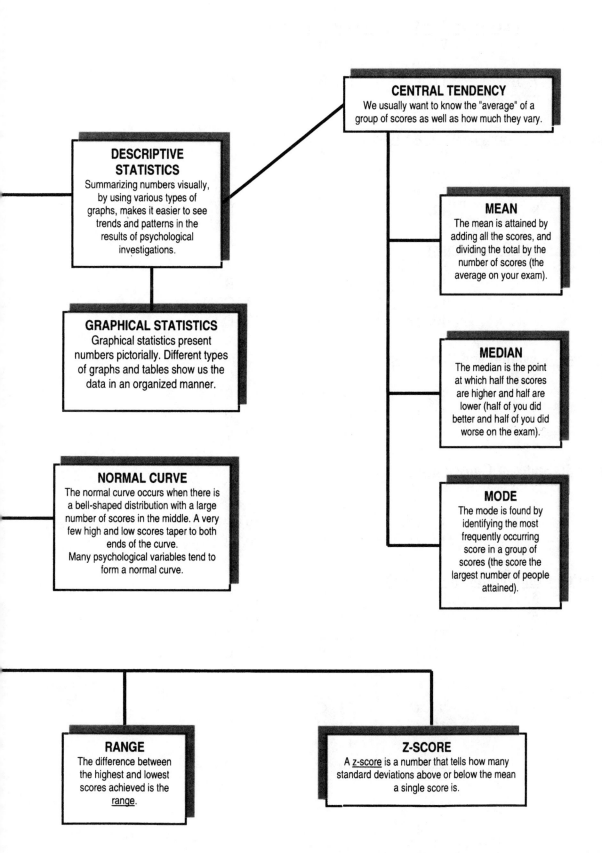

CENTRAL TENDENCY
We usually want to know the "average" of a group of scores as well as how much they vary.

DESCRIPTIVE STATISTICS
Summarizing numbers visually, by using various types of graphs, makes it easier to see trends and patterns in the results of psychological investigations.

MEAN
The mean is attained by adding all the scores, and dividing the total by the number of scores (the average on your exam).

GRAPHICAL STATISTICS
Graphical statistics present numbers pictorially. Different types of graphs and tables show us the data in an organized manner.

MEDIAN
The median is the point at which half the scores are higher and half are lower (half of you did better and half of you did worse on the exam).

NORMAL CURVE
The normal curve occurs when there is a bell-shaped distribution with a large number of scores in the middle. A very few high and low scores taper to both ends of the curve.
Many psychological variables tend to form a normal curve.

MODE
The mode is found by identifying the most frequently occurring score in a group of scores (the score the largest number of people attained).

RANGE
The difference between the highest and lowest scores achieved is the range.

Z-SCORE
A z-score is a number that tells how many standard deviations above or below the mean a single score is.

ANSWERS TO PRACTICE EXAMS

Chapter 1: Introduction to Psychology and Research Methods
1. C	5. B	9. B	13. B	17. A
2. D	6. C	10. A	14. A	18. B
3. B	7. B	11. C	15. B	19. C
4. C	8. C	12. A	16. B	20. A

Chapter 2: The Brain, Biology, and Behavior
1. B	5. D	9. C	13. A	17. A
2. D	6. C	10. C	14. D	18. A
3. C	7. C	11. A	15. C	19. A
4. D	8. A	12. C	16. B	20. D

Chapter 3: Child Development
1. B	5. D	9. B	13. C	17. A
2. B	6. A	10. B	14. B	18. B
3. D	7. B	11. A	15. A	19. C
4. C	8. A	12. D	16. D	20. D

Chapter 4: Sensation and Perception
1. D	5. B	9. D	13. C	17. C
2. A	6. D	10. A	14. A	18. B
3. C	7. A	11. C	15. C	19. B
4. B	8. D	12. B	16. C	20. D

Chapter 5: States of Consciousness
1. A	5. A	9. B	13. B	17. D
2. B	6. C	10. C	14. B	18. C
3. C	7. B	11. C	15. B	19. C
4. B	8. C	12. C	16. D	20. B

Chapter 6: Conditioning and Learning
1. D	5. D	9. C	13. B	17. D
2. B	6. C	10. D	14. B	18. C
3. D	7. C	11. A	15. C	19. A
4. D	8. C	12. B	16. B	20. C

Chapter 7: Memory
1. B	5. B	9. C	13. C	17. C
2. D	6. B	10. C	14. C	18. D
3. D	7. A	11. A	15. D	19. A
4. B	8. B	12. D	16. B	20. A

Chapter 8: Cognition, Language, and Creativity
1. A	5. D	9. B	13. B	17. C
2. D	6. A	10. C	14. B	18. C
3. B	7. D	11. A	15. B	19. B
4. C	8. B	12. A	16. D	20. D

Chapter 9: Motivation and Emotion
1. D	5. C	9. A	13. C	17. D
2. B	6. C	10. C	14. A	18. C
3. B	7. B	11. A	15. D	19. B
4. C	8. B	12. C	16. A	20. D

Chapter 10: Personality
1. B	5. C	9. B	13. C	17. C
2. B	6. D	10. D	14. D	18. C
3. A	7. A	11. C	15. D	19. D
4. B	8. B	12. B	16. B	20. D

Chapter 11: Health, Stress, and Coping
1. A	5. C	9. D	13. C	17. A
2. A	6. D	10. C	14. A	18. D
3. C	7. A	11. D	15. C	19. A
4. A	8. B	12. B	16. A	20. D

Chapter 12: Psychological Disorders
1. B	5. B	9. B	13. C	17. A
2. A	6. C	10. B	14. D	18. D
3. A	7. C	11. A	15. B	19. A
4. C	8. A	12. D	16. B	20. D

Chapter 13: Therapies
1. C	5. B	9. C	13. A	17. D
2. C	6. B	10. C	14. A	18. D
3. A	7. A	11. C	15. A	19. C
4. D	8. D	12. C	16. C	20. A

Chapter 14: Social Behavior
1. B	5. A	9. B	13. D	17. A
2. C	6. D	10. C	14. C	18. B
3. D	7. B	11. C	15. C	19. C
4. C	8. B	12. B	16. A	20. B